W9-ARK-279

FUN WITH

Terrarium Gardening

Virginie and George A. Elbert

CROWN PUBLISHERS, INC., NEW YORK

© *1973 by Virginie and George A. Elbert*
All rights reserved. No part of this book may
be reproduced or utilized in any form or by
any means, electronic or mechanical, including
photocopying, recording, or by any information
storage and retrieval system, without permission
in writing from the Publisher.

Inquiries should
be addressed to Crown Publishers, Inc.,
419 Park Avenue South, New York, N.Y. 10016

Library of Congress Catalog Card Number: 72-96664
Printed in the United States of America
Published simultaneously in Canada by
General Publishing Company Limited
Designed by Ruth Smerechniak

Fourth Printing, August, 1974

Contents

1

An Introduction
to Terrariums

How Terrariums Started

In the summer of 1829 Dr. Nathaniel Ward, a London physician, planted the chrysalis of an adult Sphinx Moth in ordinary garden soil within a closed glass container, with the object of observing its emergence. As most soils do, this contained seeds and spores which promptly germinated. Dr. Ward expected the plantlets to die off immediately in their "airless" container. Instead, he was startled to observe that they continued to live and grow in perfect health. And, as this was contrary to the scientific belief at the time—that plants must have ventilation to survive—he soon became more interested in their behavior than in the original purpose of his experiment. Here was undeniable evidence that plants could exist in a hermetically sealed container. The wonder of it was that this particular lot flourished without attention for four years.

Dr. Ward then experimented with larger containers and various other plants with even better results. For instance, he found that tropical foliage plants did particularly well. One of his cases carried on for fifteen years . . . tightly closed all the time. Based on his reports, decorative units were manufactured which came to be known as Wardian Cases. Planted with greenery, they were a feature of nineteenth century drawing rooms.

The plants flourished in a tightly closed container because the moisture in the soil never evaporated and the air within was recycled by the plants. The success of the system depended on the soil's containing just the right amount of moisture. Too much, and the soil became waterlogged with consequent rotting of the plants. Too little, and the plants would simply dry out.

True Wardian Cases have become rare nowadays. They were ideal where coolish temperatures prevailed. Victorian homes were freezing by our standards, and one of the reasons the plants did so well in the cases was that they were partly protected against extreme temperature drops at night. Plant material was confined to a few indestructibles. For a while Wardian Cases were used as a kind of miniature greenhouse for orchids, most of which delight in cool temperatures. But in the modern home, with its wide range of temperatures, and with our preference for warmth in winter, results were not satisfactory. Wardian Cases became death chambers when the thermometer rose into the eighties and nineties. American sunlight through the glass was lethal. And if you were to put a lamp over the closed glass tank during a warm spell, the plants would rot away.

Now we have no trouble growing tropical foliage plants near a window, so the Wardian Case offers no advantage. And if we want to raise the tenderer, blooming plants, with or without artificial light, we are obliged to compromise. Our terrariums are a modification of Dr. Ward's principle.

What Is a Terrarium?

The modern terrarium is any transparent vessel, with a cover or a small opening at the top, that contains soil and growing plants. Under this definition even bottles pass muster, the only problem being the extreme narrowness of the opening, which requires special techniques of planting and care. The terrarium can be just a setting for potted plants in an arrangement. In which case, when kept partly covered, a humid microclimate is created. As long as there is enough soil for the plants and enough moisture to maintain them, terrarium conditions are met. There are no limits in size—except cost and practicality. They range from 3-inch balls or cubes, containing a single tiny plant, to such large showpieces as the "Aquadome," illustrated on p. 64.

The word terrarium originally described a round glass bowl—really a much reduced Wardian Case, in which mosses and small woodland plants, such as Princess Pine, Wintergreen, Partridgeberry, Rattlesnake Plantain, and ferns were gathered together in the fall and provided some cheerful growing greenery and red berries in the house during winter. Our aversion to stripping the woods of these plants has led to a decline in the popularity of such plantings.

With the introduction of much tropical and desert foliage and many blooming plants of small size, a new era for the terrarium has begun. We are now using a greater variety of plant material than formerly and our terrariums are more decorative. To house the plants we use glass and plastic vessels of varied and attractive shapes. All our planters, like the original terrariums, have an opening which we keep covered or partly uncovered, depending on the needs of the plants inside. We can set the gardens near a window, or suspend fluorescent lights over them and grow small blooming plants.

Variety of plants has been at the expense of uniformity of growing conditions. Dr. Ward's plants all had to be compatible. Ours are much less so. We do not mix cacti and ferns, to be sure, but we do have plants in the same terrarium that demand differing amounts of watering, ventilation, humidity, and light. We try to strike an average between them, and that is far easier if we can open the cover partway or even remove it completely from time to time. And we want to be able to water one plant and not another. Our plants are faster growing than Dr. Ward's purposely sluggish choices, and though they are not encouraged to spread themselves, we must replace them more often and groom them for appearance' sake.

We are no longer dependent on window light for growth. This is fortunate in our cities, where light is reduced by smog and by the shadows of other buildings. Fluorescent lighting and longer hours of illumination provide us with the means of using blooming plants as never before.

So terrarium planting and growing has become a very different art. It is an art just in its infancy but rapidly growing in popularity. Under controlled conditions, terrariums can still occasionally be sealed off from the air for long periods of time without damage to the plants. How to go about choosing a container, planting, and growing the new way is the subject of this book.

Why a Terrarium?

Most people like terrariums because they are good looking. It is as simple as that. Even the most gracelessly put together planting is a unit; a little island of greenery protected within its glass or plastic shell—much like a painting in a shadowbox. It is a sort of vase where the flowers, instead of sticking out of the top and lasting but a few days, are contained within and go on living for a long time. The gleam of the vessel and the green of the plants go well on a sideboard, end table, or coffee table—even in an unused fireplace. In short, it is a piece of natural furniture.

The terrarium needs relatively little attention. It is not like a

potted plant, requiring daily watering and trimming, soon outgrow-
ing itself or dying.

You will find out that plants prefer living in this microclimate.
The glass sides and covering protect them from drafts and sudden
changes of temperature. They are only disturbed at long intervals.
They like that. Inside the bowl or tank the humidity is contained
and runs much higher than in the living areas of houses or apartments (80 percent, as against 20 to 30 percent). This is ideal for
plants, even cacti and succulents.

Because so many of their basic needs are satisfied, plants need less
light under terrarium conditions. With its regularity and long hours,
compared to natural daylight with its alternation of cloudy days, the
relatively weak fluorescent tube supplies ideal illumination for
growth. In the city, plants suffer from the effects of aerial pollution.
In the terrarium they are at least partly protected. That makes a big
difference these days. As far as the plants are concerned, it is a peace-
able kingdom, and they respond by growing slowly and healthily.
If you have a difficult or tender plant, put it in a terrarium and it
will flourish as nowhere else. Finally, it is a perfect refuge for plants
from cats and inquisitive children. If you have either, you will have
to grow your plants in a terrarium.

Now that terrariums have become popular, there are many handsome containers being manufactured just for this purpose. And for
those who like to go it alone, the plastic stores and glassware departments of department stores are full of beautiful goblets, vases, urns,
bottles, and bell jars, which can be put to this use.

All you need, is to know how to plant a terrarium—and take care
of it. All living things need care in order to achieve beauty and, in
spite of the favorable environment, terrarium plants are no exception. Terrarium growing is simple but not foolproof. In the following
pages we describe and illustrate the basic operations involved.

Although the plantings shown in the photographs farther back in
this book involve fewer complications than the big tank with which
we start, we have chosen this basic tank to illustrate most if not all
the operations involved. If you have learned and practiced these
techniques, you will be able to handle all the other problems which
may arise—and go on to improvements of your own.

A Glass and Stainless Steel Aquarium

Indoor gardeners are fortunate that the tropical fish hobby is so
popular. Aquarium tanks are perfectly adapted to terrarium use and,
because of large production and distribution, are among the least
expensive transparent containers available. Aquarium shapes are excellent for our purpose.

For our step-by-step demonstration of the planting of a large ter-

Glass and stainless steel tank with a capacity of 20 gallons, and measuring 24″ × 12″ × 16″. The bottom is a sheet of slate. This is a very useful size with a two-tube, 24-inch fluorescent fixture.

rarium we chose this glass and stainless steel aquarium, identified as 20-gallon size, and measuring 24″ x 12″ x 16″. The frame is of stainless steel. The glass sides are cemented to the inside of the frame. The bottom is a sheet of slate.

Following are the sizes of stainless steel aquariums produced by the largest manufacturer, Metaframe Corporation, Slater Drive, East Paterson, New Jersey 07407. (They also make all-glass terrariums.)

		L. W. H.			L. W. H.
2	Gallons	10″ x 6″ x 8″	20	"	20″ x 12″ x 12″
2½	"	12″ x 6″ x 8″	23	"	30″ x 12″ x 14″
3½	"	14″ x 7″ x 9″	26	"	30″ x 12″ x 16″
5	"	14″ x 8″ x 10″	29	"	30″ x 12″ x 18″
5½	"	16″ x 8″ x 10″	30	"	36″ x 13″ x 16″
8	"	18″ x 9″ x 11″	40	"	36″ x 14″ x 18″
10	"	20″ x 10″ x 12″	50	"	36″ x 18″ x 18″
13½	"	20″ x 10″ x 16″	55	"	48″ x 13″ x 20″
10	"	24″ x 8″ x 12″	70	"	48″ x 18″ x 20″
15	"	24″ x 12″ x 12″	100	"	60″ x 18″ x 20″
20	"	24″ x 12″ x 16″	125	"	72″ x 18″ x 20″

Recently the manufacturers of tropical fish tanks have found a way to seal the glass panes so that a metal frame has become unnecessary. The all-glass containers are five sided, as the bottom is also of glass, and are set in a narrow wooden base. Ambassador All Glass Aquariums and Metaframe Corporation are leaders in producing them.

All-glass aquariums are more ornamental than those with steel supports. We did not use one for our demonstration only because the metal frame shows up more clearly on our photographs.

Before the appearance of all-glass aquariums, attempts were made to use Plexiglas sheeting. They were many times more expensive than the glass aquariums and, unless flawlessly crafted, were likely to warp. A permanent disadvantage of all plastic for our purposes is that it scratches easily. Grit and acids in the soil rapidly roughen the surface of plastic, interfering with its perfect transparency. In small sizes, straight sided, made to order or handmade, plastic terrariums can be very attractive, and when it is possible to mold them they become considerably cheaper than those made of fused sheets. Some very good looking and practical terrariums in other, more easily molded shapes, are already available and growing in popularity.

Utensils

Here we've laid out some of the utensils which you will be using when building any kind of terrarium.

The watering can has a long thin spout. This has two advantages. When your terrarium is completed and is provided with a cover glass, and may even have a fluorescent fixture above it, the narrow spout permits you to water the plants through small openings in the cover and to reach plants in every corner of your garden. Since the water pours out in a narrow stream, it is not forceful enough to wash down light soil and will permit you to limit the amount of water being given to each of the plants.

Long-spouted watering can, bowl for mixing, and cup for measuring. The spoons are for stirring and digging holes. The brush is for cleaning up when the terrarium planting is done.

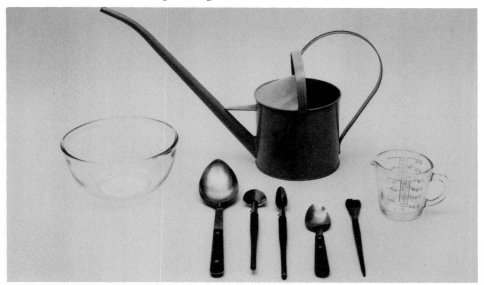

The mixing bowl could be any large vessel. It's just a reminder that you need one. For a terrarium of the size we are building, it should be much larger. This one we will have to refill a few times. We use it for mixing our "soil."

The cup serves to measure out just the right amount of each ingredient in the foundation soil mix.

With the big spoon, which comes from our kitchen set, we stir the materials of the mix together and transfer the soil to the terrarium. The smaller tablespoon serves to dig out smaller holes or transfer smaller amounts of soil than the big one.

The two narrow spoons with long handles are part of an indoor gardening set of a kind that is available in housewares departments and Japanese variety stores. There is sometimes a rake in such sets for which we have found no use in terrarium work. These two are really small shovels, ideal for working plants out of pots of various sizes, or digging narrow deep holes in the soil.

The brush is of soft camel's hair for cleaning up the terrarium after the work is done. It is soft enough to brush leaves without damaging them. It can be bought either in an art or hardware-paint store.

Small round and square plastic pots for terrarium planting.

Pots

The use of pots is an innovation of the modern terrarium. They are unthinkable in the "natural" planting of wild forest greenery, which is only expected to last a season. And, until recently, they were considered improper for any terrarium planting.

Of course a pot won't do if the terrarium is tiny, or if the opening does not permit its passage. But it is such a practical solution to many terrarium problems that we use one wherever we can.

The old method of removing a plant from its pot and setting it in terrarium soil always causes some damage, if only temporary. If, as is usually the case, the plant must be handled a good deal as you move it around in developing your scene, the plant inevitably suffers. Especially our modern blooming plants are very sensitive to rough handling. Leaving them in their pots insures their arrival in their new home in tiptop shape.

An unpotted plant in a terrarium soon spreads its roots in every direction. No objection—until the moment when it is advisable to replace it, either because it has grown too big or has suffered some setback which makes it unsightly. Then you will find that hauling out the roots wrecks your landscape completely . . . not only destroying its contours but uprooting other plants in the process. Not only is this major surgery harmful to all the plants but it becomes exceedingly difficult to reconstitute the planting. It is a simple matter to lift out a pot and replace it with another. The plant suffers no disturbance whatsoever any more than those already in the terrarium.

When we use a variety of plants, their culture will differ somewhat, one from the other. Some we will want to water or fertilize more, some less. Plants rooted in the communal soil must all receive the same treatment. Not so when they are in pots. Then each one can be given some individual attention.

Incidentally, you can prevent roots from growing through the holes in the bottom of your pots by covering them on the inside with a small piece of plastic screening. And it is also worth noting that you need place no crock or pebble drainage in the bottoms. They just waste space and, in a terrarium, contribute not at all to the health of the plants.

Still another advantage of a pot is that you are able to control the angling of your plant in your "landscape" far better. You can move the pot any way you like and the plant simply moves with it. If you try to do the same thing with a rooted plant you can easily damage it.

The pots we use are invariably of plastic. They are lighter and thinner walled, taking up less space. And they retain moisture much longer than a clay pot.

The pot sizes most often used are:

> 1½" to 2" square or round
> 2¾" to 3"   "   "   "
> 4"   "   "   "

Tiny plants with little root and small-leaved creepers do not need pots.

Rocks and pebbles.

Rocks and Pebbles

For creating a terrarium landscape you will need rocks and pebbles of various sizes. The large irregular ones in the photo are from quarries in Franklin, New Jersey, which is famous for its variety of minerals. We picked them up partly out of our interest in minerals, partly to use in our terrariums. They fracture unequally and are rather like certain weathered large boulders. Also they are streaked with crystals and areas of different colors and reflections. Such larger rocks are used to buttress the hills and cliffs, to hide the pots or to be a beautiful feature in their own right.

Smooth large rocks are rarely used. Lacking sharp edges they do not grip the soil and therefore are hard to keep in place. Also they do not usually suggest the stony parts of a landscape. Big, rough, many-angled stones add a great deal to the variety of your scene and contrast well with the greenery.

Tropical fish stores sell interesting rocks which are used in building the scenery of aquariums. Mineral and lapidary stores often have bins of rocks that are not up to exhibit quality. But the best way is to pick them up yourself in the country whenever you have the opportunity. Quarries are always a good source. We get beautiful snow-white crystalline stones from limestone quarries, for instance. Also keep an eye out for slag. There are many kinds that are porous and pitted, and others that are colored and glassy.

Smaller stones are also used. The flat ones help support larger ones or fill spaces between them. Colorful ones come in handy as fillers and for decorating a bare area between plants.

The round small stones are Japanese pebbles which are sold by the box in different colors, usually white, black, or brown. We find them ideal for covering flat areas in the landscape and as a contrast to our sharply angled rocks. The black ones can give the effect of a shaded pool or a deep valley. The whites suggest clear water or a beach. Other types of pebbles can be used for the same purposes.

We do not use decorative pieces of wood—driftwood, for instance —in our foundation plantings, because the moisture in the terrarium causes it to rot and such wood usually harbors insect life. Occasionally we will place wood shapes on the surface of the mix or incorporate them into the elements of an arrangement where it is likely to do the least damage.

Basic ingredients of houseplant mixes. Clockwise, starting at upper left —vermiculite, peat moss, limestone, perlite.

The Soil Ingredients

We use two different, closely related, soil formulas in the terrarium. One is the mix we prefer for growing all our houseplants. The other is the soil for building up the landscape. Neither of them contains natural garden soil.

In garden loam there usually lives a menagerie of pests that would have a field day killing off the plants in your terrarium. You *can* get rid of them by sterilizing the soil before using it—but it's a messy business, as the only way to do it is in the kitchen oven. Packaged houseplant loam is sterilized, to be sure, but has a heavy consistency and the particles are too fine for most of our plants. Unless we make tests with special equipment we have no way of knowing the chemical content and activity of such soils. Of the packaged mixes available in the stores much the best in our opinion are the Black Magic mixes and Baccto Potting Soil.

The modern indoor grower much prefers a soilless mix, as it is called, made up of peat moss, perlite, and vermiculite, and uses it for all of his plants. It is sterile, very light, gritty, and water retentive. We know its approximate chemical behavior (it has a pH * of about 6, if you are interested), and if it is too acid we have a simple means of remedying it. We can make up our proportions to suit the plants. We find that they grow well in it. The separate ingredients come in packages that can be handled and stored without trouble. Because it does not become soggy and can be kept light and just moist, it also makes an ideal soil for the landscape of your indoor garden.

We will describe these ingredients in the order in which they are *always* listed in mix formulas.

PEAT MOSS

Peat moss is the partly decomposed remains (sounds awful, doesn't it?) of certain bog plants, principally sedge and sphagnum moss. The peat from sphagnum moss is greatly to be preferred over sedge moss as it is less coarse and acid.

Sphagnum peat moss can be purchased in variety stores and garden centers in small plastic packs, .7-cubic-foot pickup bales, and big commercial bales. If you are making a terrarium or maintain a small indoor garden the small packs will do. If your gardening is on a larger scale you will find it pays to invest in the pickup bale, which has a handle for carrying.

Peat moss supplies the fibrous, organic part of our mix. It absorbs and holds quantities of water, is light in weight, and contains a very small amount of nutriment for plants. Its particles fill up the spaces between the inorganic coarser materials.

PERLITE

Obsidian, a lava rock, when subjected to intense heat, explodes and forms the white granular substance called perlite. A trade name for it is Sponge-Rok. It takes the place of sand in the mix, being gritty and very light. It absorbs and evaporates water easily. Because the fine dust of perlite can be annoying to nose and eyes, it is a good idea to wash it in a sieve and drain well before mixing, even though it is then a little more difficult to spread.

---

* pH is an arbitrary measure of acidity or alkalinity. In the series 5 to 10, the low numbers are acid, the high ones alkaline. Neutral is 7 pH. Most houseplants are in the 6 to 8 pH range. To make a simple test, buy little rolls of litmus paper, available in tropical fish stores, bury a piece of the tape in moist soil for a few seconds and then compare the color with the chart on the cover of the tape's container.

VERMICULITE

Vermiculite is simply mica which has, like perlite, been subjected to extremely high temperatures. Mica is a mineral which is found in nature as compacted, very thin crystal sheets. The heat makes these sheets curl, separate, and expand like an accordion. The myriad of crystalline surfaces hold water only by surface tension. Mica is rather soft in texture and breaks down into fine particles after a while.

The appearance of the vermiculite should be in accordionlike cubes. There is some material on the market that is labeled horticultural vermiculite, but that is far closer to a type used as insulation in buildings. The pieces are larger and coarser, or poorly expanded, and when rubbed between the fingers immediately break down into a greasy mush. It's deadly to the plants as it contains harmful impurities.

You can buy vermiculite in variety stores and garden centers in small packs and half-bushel paper bags.

LIMESTONE

The fourth material is lime. Most of our houseplants like a neutral soil and find peat moss rather acid. This is aggravated with time by the use of fertilizers. To compensate, we add some lime. Horticultural lime comes in many forms—dolomite limestone chips, horticultural powdered lime, and eggshells for instance. We, ourselves, save the breakfast eggshells and grind them down with pestle and mortar. You may prefer to toss them into the blender for a few seconds. The proportion of lime needed is approximately a tablespoon to a quart of mix as a minimum, but most of our houseplants can use about double the amount. So you have a good deal of leeway without causing damage to your plants. Just don't fail to use it. If your water is very limey, forget about adding any more.

SPHAGNUM MOSS

Although it is not a component of our mix we want to discuss sphagnum moss here because it has a number of important special uses and you should know about it. Milled sphagnum moss, the dry, finely ground product, is used for starting seeds and there are those who use it to replace peat moss in mixes. It is the same moss whose roots, after a period of decay, end up as sphagnum peat moss. Here we will consider it in its live state or as the whole dried plant.

This moss is one of the marvels of nature. For its type it is a rather large plant and grows in immense quantities in the bogs of the temperate and northern zones. Its myriad tiny leaves contain cells that are empty and that absorb water to the amount of some twenty times its own weight. Hence it is sometimes referred to as a vegetable sponge. In the bogs it forms deep soft masses of great extent, growing best in a thin film of water. Although there are many species of sphagnum moss, there is no essential difference we know of between them, as regards their horticultural uses.

The moss can be gathered at any bog, bagged, and brought home. Kept in a plastic bag it will stay alive for a long time. The stems are often several inches in length. When packed into a covered container, watered regularly and given some light it will begin to grow and may spread more rapidly than plants which you set in it. The moss can also be dried and packaged. Whole dried sphagnum has the same uses as the live material but we have found the latter superior for most purposes.

Sphagnum moss has very little nutritive value to offer other plants, yet tropical exotics grow and bloom quite happily in it. A layer of the moss can be packed loosely into a container and plants simply poked into the soft tangle. Kept moderately moist the moss benefits the plants and their roots spread rapidly through it. We have found it particularly useful in plantings of tender miniatures—such as begonias (*B. prismatocarpa* for instance), little Sinningias, and most of the trailing gesneriads. For the cultivation of carnivorous plants it is absolutely essential. However, landscaping with it is difficult. Its tiny leaves stick to the glass and the plant refuses to stay in one place. Its decorative usage is therefore confined to plants you cannot grow any other way.

Formula for Houseplant Potting Soil

We will tell you about our *potting* mix first. (The *terrarium* foundation mix for building your landscape is described in the next section.) Every plant in your terrarium should first be potted in this mix— until a better one comes along. And please ignore all advice about using humus, rotted leaves, sand collected in the country, and other "natural" materials. They may be more romantic but they don't work as well. Not being uniform you can't control them in the way you can a soilless mix.

If you have bought a plant potted in ordinary soil, give it a few days of rest, making sure that it has recovered from its transportation to a new environment—which will be indicated by the appearance of new growth. Then knock it out of the pot, wash the roots gently in a bowl of lukewarm water to remove all the old soil, and repot in our mix. Doing this will save you endless future trouble. Allow the plant another rest of several days before setting it in a terrarium.

The formula is: 1 part peat moss (1 cup)
                       1 part perlite (1 cup)
                       1 part vermiculite (1 cup)
                       1 tablespoon crushed eggshell or limestone
                         chips to each three cups of mix.

This is easy, but watch out for the peat moss. It is compacted in the bale and must be broken up and fluffed. It is in this latter state that it should be measured against the other ingredients. By the way, do not allow your peat moss to dry out completely in the package. It will be much easier to handle if you keep it moist by adding some water and closing the bag until you are ready to use it.

Formula and Mixing of the Foundation Soil

We have already described the potting mix and its components. We use the same materials without the lime (though it would do no harm) in compounding our foundation mix.

Mixing the foundation soil. The cup contains vermiculite. In the bowl are peat moss on the left, and perlite on the right.

FOUNDATION MIX

2 parts peat moss
3 parts perlite
3 parts vermiculite
2 parts water (1½ parts if the perlite is already moistened. See p. 15.)

Translate the parts into cups of the materials and you have a proportion of *eight cups of soil to two cups of water*. This is so important because it gives you the exact amount of water required— something you are not likely to hit upon by yourself, the first time out. In fact it is almost impossible for a beginner to avoid wetting the soil excessively. The precise proportion of water is essential because it controls the whole balance of the terrarium. Knowing this proportion you will be less likely to water too much once the terrarium is operating. The amount in *potting mixes* varies with the requirements of different plants.

In the illustration we are using a somewhat larger bowl than the one in the photograph on page 10, and more in proportion to our needs for a large terrarium. To the left in the bowl is the peat moss, to the right the perlite, and in the cup is the vermiculite.

This mix is used as the anchor for our pots in many kinds of terrariums. The larger amount of perlite in the mix is unsightly at first, but this snow-white material soon discolors in contact with the peat moss.

Pour the dry ingredients into the bowl and stir thoroughly together.

Fill your watering can with as many cups of water as you will need for the quantity of dry mix you have measured out. Draw the water lukewarm from the warm water faucet. There is less chlorine present and warm water mixes in more rapidly. Alternatively you can fill the can and measure the water in the cup as you pour it into the mix.

Pour slowly, mixing constantly, until all the water is absorbed. Then keep stirring until it is evenly distributed through the mass. In mixing dry soils with water, small amounts at the bottom or sides of a bowl may remain dry unless they are carefully scraped and stirred in.

The soil will be just barely moist to the touch. It may seem altogether too dry to you; but don't worry, it is just right to create a humid atmosphere for the plants, once the terrarium is closed. Remember, you are not providing moist soil for the plants. That is already in the pots. All you are doing is creating the environment. If you have overwatered, large drops will congeal on the glass when the terrarium is covered.

If the soil were moister it would pack better and would be easier to handle while you are building your landscape. However, the soil will settle down in the terrarium soon enough, and the main thing is to have the right moisture conditions at the start. Whether you work with small or large terrariums the amount of water and mix remains the same—two and eight.

2 🌿

Building
a Basic Terrarium

Preparing the Terrarium

Your first step is to clean the glass panes of the tank. Manufacturers' labels may need to be removed, and there is usually a fine film of dust on the surfaces. Do not use any caustic or abrasive materials on labels. Soak them with water and work them loose with a sponge. To put a brilliant finish on the outside of the glass, use a sponge soaked in a mild solution of ammonia or vinegar. But do not use either on the inside of the tank.

Drainage

A true Wardian Case is hermetically sealed, never evaporates and never needs watering, so that drainage material seems superfluous. The same can be said of a terrarium if we keep it closed, which we can do with some very slow growing foliage plants. However, in our modern terrarium we are likely to use many different kinds of plants, some of which, without attention, would become unsightly. And though these may need hardly any watering, others soon dry out in our foundation mix. Furthermore, as we have already pointed out, the cover of the terrarium must be left open during warm periods in the house caused either by weather outside or by central heating. So some of our plants do need watering from time to time and the whole terrarium occasionally needs replenishing of its moisture.

In watering we must be very moderate but it is difficult to avoid some excess which would be dangerous for the plants if allowed to stagnate in the foundation mix. An ounce of prevention is therefore advisable.

As the terrarium planting ages, the soil settles and packs down because of waterings and its own weight. The compressed foundation mix is no longer as well aerated as at the beginning.

For these reasons it is advisable to lay down a thin layer of drainage material.

As the first step in building any terrarium planting, spread one inch of perlite on the bottom. If it is dry, dribble it in slowly to prevent dust from rising, which is not only uncomfortable for you but puts a film on the glass. If you have moistened it, dab it into place. It is rather sticky in this state, but manageable. Spread it evenly.

You can substitute limestone chips or just plain pebbles, but these have the disadvantage of adding weight. Plastic chips would be better. We must try to keep our terrarium as light as possible so that it can be handled easily.

In our illustration the dark area in the corner is the slate bottom of the terrarium and indicates the depth of the perlite.

Drainage. Perlite is laid down first.

Planning

It is pretty obvious that you can't go off into abstract fantasies about how you will plant your garden. Except for having more experience to draw on for a vague notion, we have as blank a mind as anyone else about what we are going to have in the way of a landscape. The ideas have to develop out of the plants and materials you have available. Observing their sizes and relationships automatically leads to some rudimentary conception. And, as you are working and trying things out a more definite idea emerges almost automatically. So, before proceeding any further, you should gather together enough plants and rocks of a practical size and appearance so that you will have as much freedom of choice as possible. Often the nucleus of a design is some favorite plant you have picked out for the purpose and all the others, as well as the rocks and pebbles, are chosen in relation to it.

In laying out a terrarium planting you have to conform to the space and shape limitations of the container. For instance, in a round terrarium your design is of necessity concentric, since everything has to work inward from the glass. Look over your plants and decide which ones will fit into the area and approximately how many you need to work with. Then visualize some sort of arrangement that is pleasing.

In a small terrarium one attractive plant may be sufficient. A somewhat larger container may hold two or three, and you will need to consider whether they can grow together in the same environment and whether they look well together.

However a large tank like ours calls for even more careful planning as it will not do just to dig in several plants on the same level. The way we secure variety in the scene is by contouring the soil, using various size stones, and choosing plants that offer contrasts in size and coloring.

You can construct quite realistic little landscapes, including figurines, bridges, lanterns, and so on, which are the stock-in-trade of minor Japanese crafts. These are fun but not very well suited to modern decoration or furniture, being rather old-fashioned in feeling. However, if you like this kind of literalness you will find, in our list of suppliers, firms which carry such accessories.

Our own way is to use the plants we have and arrange the contours, rocks, and plants in a manner which is as varied as possible. We try to create a miniature landscape in keeping with the tropical exotics that grow best in this terrarium environment. We don't strive for realism. The end effect is intended to be an artificial scene, with plants, hills, valleys, and cliffs—a decorative stage setting rather than a real scene.

In most cases it is best to plan for one view of the terrarium—usually a frontal one. If your tank is set in a position where it has to be seen from the narrow end, the principle will be the same with a switch in design of 90° and a deeper narrower landscape.

Usually, if all the plants are set on one level they will obscure each other, and the only interesting view will be from above. If that is the viewing point it will do. However, the way to make the most of your planting space and to create the greatest variety is to have as many different levels as possible. By terracing the vertical spaces and placing the rocks strategically, you will accomplish this and make room for more plants that will stand out individually as well as taking part in the design.

Thus an essential feature from the viewer's position is a frontal area which is as low as possible and rear or sides which are at some point(s) as high as possible. In between are terraces or declivities.

From the very nature of this plan, the low area suggests a watercourse, pond, or meadow, and the higher parts, hills and mountains. By ingenuity in the arrangement of these features, and of your various rocks, you can create an infinite number of designs which depend as much on the plants used as on the shape of the terrain.

Here are a few general plans:

1. The low area extends right across the front, and the rear rises in irregular terraces to a more or less even upper level. This is a good idea for collections of small upright and trailing plants.

2. A low level in the center, surrounded by high points.

3. The lower level, which can be anywhere in front, extends into and between "mountains" reaching nearly to the back of the terrarium. The valley can be straight or angled; on one level or continuously rising. Through narrowing the sides and the use of stones of decreasing size, some effect of false perspective can be achieved.

4. The high point can be to the right, the left, or center, with terraced lower areas between. Contouring the scene is part of the fun.

This is what is involved in laying down your foundation and building the deeper areas of mix to hold your plants.

Outlining the Design in Charcoal

We did not list charcoal among our basic ingredients because we use it neither as drainage nor as part of the mix. If need be, though, it can replace perlite for the former purpose. Charcoal can be bought as packaged chips from a tropical fish store.

For the next step we use charcoal because of its black color. Outlining and then covering with charcoal the areas we intend to build as the higher parts of our planned landscape helps us to visualize the design more efficiently. The black stands out starkly against the white, and the edge serves as a guide to placing soil accurately. Any

Charcoal spread over the white perlite indicates where the higher parts of the terrarium garden are to be built.

contrasting colored pebbles of small size will do. Without this aid you can easily become uncertain of your plan as you work with the soil and are likely to end up moving masses around without settling on anything definite. The charcoal *forces* you to make a decision right at the start. And once you have laid down the outline you can proceed with more confidence.

In our picture we have covered one part of the low area with charcoal and outlined the rest. The white area behind the line will now also be covered with charcoal. Where it is laid on solidly, we will build our soil foundation. We have chosen a central front view with high sections on either side and a valley curving to the right.

The smaller and narrower the spaces reserved for hills (black in the photograph), the steeper they must be. The larger they are the easier it will be to use terraces, and the greater the number of plants that can be accommodated. There is no rule to follow here. It is not a good idea to crowd a terrarium with plants. And a steep terrain with fewer plants can be as interesting as a more gradual slope with many plants.

Laying Down the First Soil Layer

Spread the first couple of inches of soil exactly over the charcoal covered areas. Do it by handfuls, dribbling along the boundary line first and then building up behind it. As the bright white base is very useful in calculating proportions and heights in your design, try not to darken it. If, nevertheless, some mix falls into the area, spread a

Laying the base
of foundation
soil.

very thin coat of perlite over it to restore the color.

Do not add water at this stage. Do not compact the soil in any way. It should be just as loose as it was in the bowl.

The soil has been built up to a high point on the left and depressions indicate where we might place plants and terraces. The steepest section is at the end of the valley. The area to the right is just an even slope for the present.

Building Up the Soil

Now you can begin to build up the sides of your landscape. The soil must slope generally *downward* from the glass walls in this or any design where the lowest level is central. If your high points are central the soil can slope downward *toward* the walls. But, almost invariably, it is a good plan to have it turn upward *slightly* as it approaches the glass. This gives an effect of visual continuity rather than the appearance of being cut off arbitrarily.

Since the left side has been assigned more space it will be the higher point. Where the perlite lower level approaches the glass at the rear, the space for the soil narrows. There you are obliged to build lower or the whole mass will avalanche forward. When working with soil, we see that the shape of the mounds is very much dictated by the space they occupy.

The pile in the left corner has almost reached its proper height. We must not forget to leave room at the top for a plant to grow. Some depressions have been tentatively poked into the mass, indicating where we may place our plants. No matter how much experience you have, plants being different in appearance and proportion on the shelf from in a terrarium, you will have to do some guessing as to just how much space they will occupy and which one will look best. Only after you have set the pot in place will you be sure that a plant fits into the design. However there is great room for flexibility, since position in the landscape and the rocks you will use can be shifted freely to attain some sort of symmetry. If you use a simple design and experiment with your plants you will find a pleasing arrangement.

The shape of the right-hand section is not clear as yet and is rather undifferentiated. That is partly imposed by its shape.

If we are to build any higher with this loose material we must now use stones to buttress the walls; otherwise, every time we touch the soil there will be a small avalanche encroaching on the lower level.

Placing the First Stones

We are now marshaling our stones and trying them out for size and position. Have plenty of stones in reserve. You will discover that your first placings do little more than give you a feeling for the proportions. Nine times out of ten you will have to change them around.

Four larger rocks have been set temporarily in place. Three of these buttress the steepest parts of the clifflike border of the white base. A fourth is placed on the left side near the top because we know that there will be a plant behind it and we want to see if our mound is high enough and whether this particular rock will look well there. Placing the stones gives you a feel for the spacings— where plants can go, and how big they can be.

The rocks are all colorful, without being artificial or garish. The

Three rocks are set strategically to prevent soil from falling into the valley and as points of reference for the rest of the design. The large rock high on the left gives structure to the top of the mountain and may hide a pot eventually.

In a miniature landscape these rocks look like huge boulders and rock faces. The one at the top was picked because it has vertical sides and is clifflike. The lower one slants off into the base.

At this stage we are experimenting and may have to change the choice and position of the rocks a number of times. Little depressions show us where we think a plant might go. The high point in the corner is an obvious place.

ones inside the terrarium are full of flecks and squarish crystalline forms. The two pieces in front of the case to the right are forms of tremolite, one being banded with pink and orange stripes and the other crystalline white. All these rocks will glitter under a bright light. Glass cullet and colored slags are often as attractive as natural stones.

Digging the First Hole

The first hole for the first pot can be dug anywhere in the landscape. But Jinny has chosen the left rear corner because it will be the highest spot. Since it goes into an angle close to the glass we know that there will be no need for much shifting. If it were out in an open area it would be difficult to judge within an inch or two just where a plant will fit best in relation to those which we will use later.

The long-handled, narrow-spaded, indoor gardening tool is ideal. Soil is being piled on the side of the hole as it will probably be necessary to make a loftier hill. In fact, from the outside it is pretty obvious that this is the case. The bowl, partly filled with foundation mix, stands ready and the large stone has been laid aside while the digging proceeds.

The big rock has been removed temporarily and Jinny is digging a hole with the long-handled narrow shovel. As she wants the mound to stay just as high as before she is piling the soil on the side, not removing it. The bowl remains close by in case she needs additional soil.

The hole has not been made as deep as the pot. Trying it out in the corner, Jinny found that the plant would look better if the hill were a bit higher still. She is filling in soil around the pot from her hoard in the bowl next to the tank. It is carefully dribbled into place — never packed down.

The pot is now covered. Filling in around it, Jinny kept dropping soil behind so that it partly frames the plant. The plant is an *Episcia* 'Jinny Elbert,' a miniature with brown leaves and flaming orange red flowers. It is still young and will bloom profusely as it gets older without growing much bigger. It is in a 2-inch plastic pot.

Burying the Pot

The hole was not made the full depth of the pot as it was realized in time that the plant would have to be raised. Instead the soil is being dribbled all around the pot to build up the hill. Note that the plant is not set vertically in the soil but is angled forward.

The plant is an *Episcia* with brown leaves and flaming tomato-colored flowers. It is more dwarf than most of its kind and will grow very slowly. The first blooms are just opening. But, after it has been in the terrarium for a few weeks, it will settle down to continuous production. It is far better to start out with a young plant than one which has reached maturity, for it is much more likely to adapt well to the terrarium environment and has a much longer life expectancy.

Switching Rocks

The rock which originally stood on top of the hill has been replaced. We found it too heavy in appearance and too large in relation to the size of the plant. The new rocks provide more variety. By using them we get an effect of distance and height.

In order to show the foliage to the best advantage we have angled the pot forward. The leaves now fall over the rocks. If possible,

Two different rocks replace the large one we tried at first. Notice how the foliage drapes over them.

leaves should not touch the glass, and some are subject to rot if they come into contact with soil. Supporting them with the rocks keeps them clean and fresh.

It is a good idea to turn the crowns of plants toward the center of the design, or angle them along the downward ridge of a hill. It helps pull the design together and you will find yourself doing this instinctively. While working on this terrarium and analyzing our actions, we became aware that this is what we had been doing right along in all our terrarium plantings. Angling has the additional advantage of placing a plant so that it has more room to grow vertically.

The new stones form a sort of crown to the hill. Along with the plant they in no way suggest a true landscape but rather some tropical dream. If there were a huge flowering plant topping a hill, it would undoubtedly perch just as this does in its circle of rocks. And if you think of some of the enormous-leaved Philodendron species this isn't so far from reality after all.

More Rocks and an Ivy Plant

One of the limitations and challenges of terrarium planting is caused by our dependence on the plants we have in our own window or light gardens. Of course, we can go to a nursery which makes a specialty of terrarium plants and plantings. We can buy a collection

A number of rocks now surround the *Episcia,* spreading its leaves. A flat one supports one stone where the slope is steep. Notice also how the rock at the bottom of the terrarium buttresses the very steep areas of soil above it. The pot of ivy is almost buried and a few small stones frame it and support the stem at the right angle.

and follow a particular model worked out by the nursery itself. But that deprives us of half the fun and is a bit like painting pictures with printed numbered areas. Or we can wander from florist to florist picking up small plants which might be suitable. The results are often disappointing for it is difficult to judge size and shape away from the home and the container. If you do go on a shopping spree for plants, be prepared to banish some of them to the windowsill or shelf garden. Some larger ones may go into individual terrariums of their own.

The best way to start is with plants which have been around for a while and with whose appearance and habits you are thoroughly familiar. Usually we start a terrarium *because* we have a plant or two which is in just the right condition and is of the right type for the purpose. And it is around these plants that we develop our design. The idea of using the *Episcia* at one end of the terrarium and *Sinningia* 'Cindy' at the other came about in this way.

Our little *Episcia* looks much better now with a number of additional small stones, all of the same type instead of that one big one. The leaves fall naturally over them whereas over the big stone they would be held at the horizontal. The cluster makes the plant look more important and the lightness of the stones contrasts with the darkness of the leaves. The flat stone below is there to support the one above it which had a tendency to slip.

A very beautiful variegated ivy in a 2-inch pot, looking like a fantastic large-leaved tree, has been dug in next to the main hill. A pink-colored stone set right on the pot rim holds the ivy stem upright at just the angle we want. A couple of others frame the stem.

The two plants have been set in positions that are related to their height and need for light. The terrarium will go into our white-tiled, unused fireplace, where it will be lighted by a fluorescent fixture set within the flue. This illumination will keep our flowering plants blooming. The *Episcia* needs more light than the ivy, while the latter is taller. The *Episcia* will bloom and the lower leaves of the ivy will have adequate light.

The Left Side Triangle Completed

For a place just above and behind the frontal big rock we have picked a plant with flat leaves and low light requirements, *Sinningia* 'Pink Flare.' This is an everbloomer which will grow very slowly and whose flowers are of good size, held well above the foliage. It fits right into the terrace and will look magnificent when it has two or more flowers blooming at once. The flowers are a deep pink violet in color. In a terrarium this type of plant produces larger and stronger-colored flowers than outside it. We do not expect any one

Possessing a flat rosette of leaves, a miniature *Sinningia* (closely related to the Florist Gloxinia) is just right in the large flat space between the mound and the frontal rock. A tuberous plant, this one will produce its lovely trumpet flowers over a long period.

The whole terrarium before development of the right side.

of these plants to spread out and cover the surrounding soil. We are not looking for a crowded effect—but more the look of early spring.

The two flowering plants we already have in the terrarium are part of that repertory of compact flowering houseplants which are of very recent introduction to horticulture and which have made it

possible to create blooming terrariums. Illustrations further on in
this book will show you some of the others. But since we cannot
have all of them available when we need them for terrarium planting, you will have to consult our plant lists and the catalogs of modern houseplant nurserymen for a more complete idea of the numerous possibilities. These plants are far more interesting and varied
than those grown in the average outdoor garden, and once you have
tried them it is unlikely that you will ever again be interested in the
zinnia/petunia/marigold suburban-garden syndrome. These delicate
and richly colored plants are in a class by themselves.

Developing the Right Side

The right side builds up very much as did the left, except that the
slope is more gradual front to back and somewhat lower, as the area
is confined by the way the valley cuts into it. We have supported the
sides of our valley with a selection of medium-size rocks of contrasting shades.

The plant we have chosen for the peak is *Sinningia* 'Cindy.' It is
closely related to 'Pink Flare' but produces greater quantities of
flowers on a somewhat more spreading plant. This is one of the great
miniatures of modern horticulture. The flower is more than an inch
in length flaring into five lobes. The tube is purple on the outside
and white on the inside, but the throat is lined with numerous symmetrically arranged purple dots. Its habit is also more trailing than
'Pink Flare' and it tumbles partway down the hill. For this reason
it requires a somewhat elevated position.

We plant *Sinningia* 'Cindy. This prolific bloomer is set into the right
corner. This photo shows the flat supporting rocks on the left side and
the additional lead-in ones on the right.

Here we have set the fern provisionally in place. As we observe its relation to the corner plant and to 'Pink Flare,' we shift it around a bit to one side or another until we think it is properly placed, considering future spread.

Changes in the Right Side

Again we have found our original choice of rocks unsuitable. In this instance they were too small. As we built up the soil around *S.* 'Cindy,' the angle of the hill in relation to the head of the valley became steeper and our plant, because of its spread, had to be canted sharply forward. Therefore, we chose a large piece of greenish, glassy slag and set it upright directly against the pot, supported by a number of smaller ones.

Along the valley wall we placed a "boulder" of cubed crystals which supports the terrace on the right.

Adding the Begonia

The large terrace on the right calls for a more spreading plant. Miniature flowering ones would be too "busy" for this rather dramatic landscape, and would overlap each other, since the terrace does not rise much toward the back of the tank.

So we place a trimmed *Begonia richardsiana* in this spot, allowing its branches to trail over the rock placed here for just this needed support. Such a floppy plant looks uncouth at first, because the leaves lie every which way. Handling also usually disturbs these plants and it takes a while before they recover themselves. Within a week, however, it will perk up and its leaves will all face in the same direction. When moved about, plants look unsightly for a while until they reorientate themselves, assuming a symmetrical pattern. It is one of the pleasures of terrarium planting to see this take place as a plant adapts itself to its setting. Some trimming may

still be needed—a crumpled leaf or a trailing stem. Don't be afraid
to do this. Being a fairly rapid grower this Begonia will also spread
out and need disciplining from time to time. But it will remain
fairly low. *B. richardsiana* has little white flowers which it produces
with very little light.

The fern is buried. This 4-inch
fern is unique. It will never grow
taller and will spread by stolons
which are easily removed. The
cutting can be used for multiply-
ing the plant.

A Plant for the Left Side

With 'Cindy' in place and the right side developed, the left side
looked too low. Rocks and *Episcia* were raised up two inches, and
another ledge stone was added below, partially as support, partially
to break up the long sloping line of the soil.

We still need a plant in front of the hill on the left to complete
our filling of the key spots. As this hill is higher than the other, a
taller plant could be used, but we do not want one with too great
a spread as this would interfere with a view of 'Pink Flare,' perched
so neatly on its terrace. We chose a fern for its contrasting foliage.
Any small one will do. But in our experience most of the upright
types, even the tropical ones labeled as miniatures, soon grow quite
large in a terrarium. Luckily we had a very special one which was
unusually compact and spreads very slowly.

In addition to *Begonia richardsiana,* looking wilted now but soon to straighten up, we have placed another white stone strategically up the valley to bolster the hill and brighten this darker area.

This fern has an odd history. We have brought home, from near the site of an old limekiln in Connecticut, a number of pieces of porous slag which were piled out in the woods for many years. They usually have some small pieces of moss growing on them. Set in a terrarium spores present on their surfaces sprouted and soon covered the slag with masses of moss and woodland ferns. One piece produced this particular fern, which has grown beautifully for several years, spreading considerably but never reaching a height of more than 3 or 4 inches.

As consultation of botanies did not lead to identification of this fern among our native ones, we asked a botanical garden for its name. And we were astonished with the reply that it was *Nephrolepis exaltata,* commonly known as the Boston fern. However every Boston fern we have ever seen has been larger growing than this one. Be that as it may, we have propagated it so that we had plants available to use for this terrarium. Its stiff upright habit is ideal for the position.

Although you will not find this fern in the shops and will have to use one of those from our lists, at least at the start, this incident does suggest that as you get to know more about terrariums and the plants that grow well in them, you too can make discoveries of new and useful plants for the purpose. The whole subject is still in the pioneering stage.

Filling in. The flat plant in the center is *Gesneria cuneifolia* with one of the *Sinningia* 'White Sprites' on its left.

Filling-in Plants

It wouldn't do to place anything tall between the ivy and the 'Cindy.' Nor would we want anything as stiff in flower as 'Pink Flare.' *Gesneria cuneifolia* with its rosettes of long, crisp shiny green leaves and numerous, rather low, red tube flowers, was our choice. It, too, is an everbloomer and is one of the few plants that will flower profusely so low in the terrarium and so far from the fluorescent lights. It just about fills the space allotted to it and will grow slowly. Its leaves hang over the gorge in a natural way, breaking the line of the rock face and carrying the eye toward the hidden end of the valley–stream bed.

Finally, we have placed three groupings of *Sinningia pusilla* in the empty spaces near the plants. These are tiny plants with the same flower form as the other two *Sinningias*. Two of the clusters bear the normal bluish flowers while the third, up front on the left, is 'White Sprite,' a sport. *S. pusilla* has miniature tubers yet never seems to go dormant. It roots very shallowly and it is self-seeding, so that pots are not needed and new plants will soon appear in other places. If they appear in the wrong places it is easy to lift them out and shove them in somewhere else. *S. pusilla* also has the happy habit of surrounding itself with moss after a few months, adding to the realism of a woodland scene.

There are quite a number of other little ground covers which fill empty spaces in a terrarium planting, such as miniature ficus, Artillery Plant, or Baby's Tears. But none of these blooms attractively, and they are inclined to get out of hand. We like the open spaces and if too many pusillas come up we can always pot them up for our friends. Meanwhile, instead of just a green cover we will have many flowers from these little plants.

The terrarium is now finished except for a few additional stones along the sides of the valley stream and the paving of the stream bed.

Laying the Valley Floor

One by one we have set the whitish oval Japanese stones evenly down on the valley floor to create the effect of a stream without water. White though they are, they have a matte finish that does not become glaringly reflective under light. Their symmetry contrasts with the asymmetrical arrangement of almost everything else in the landscape. Far back in the valley we have placed a few of the blackish stones to create an effect of shade and distance. This illusion is increased by an imperceptible rise to the stream bed—approximately three quarters of an inch, front to back—which gives to the stone stream a down-flowing appearance.

Some of the rocks overhang the stream bed, with the flat stones going under, but not touching the bottom of the rocks, creating hollows and shadows. Still other white stones go across the face of the bordering rocks and this suggests to the eye that the rocks disappear into the "water."

The paving of the valley floor. Note the supporting stones below the Gesneria and the large rock on the left.

Looking into this view, the imagination can play all kinds of tricks with proportions and depths. This is even more striking when the terrarium is seen at a normal distance in a room rather than in the flatness of a photograph. Relative sizes suggest a gigantic landscape rather than a miniature one.

An artist friend who sat opposite this terrarium one evening seemed lost in thought. So we offered him a penny. He said that he had been making himself tiny and taking a walk in our landscape. This is the feeling you can bring to all your larger terrariums and is one of the greatest pleasures it can provide.

Cleaning up.

Cleaning Up the Stones and Plants

Now our camel's hair brush comes into play as Jinny carefully sweeps dirt from the top of the pebbles into the crevices between them or up the sides of the slopes. Bits of soil have collected on leaves during planting. Our brush is soft enough to remove these without damage to the plants. Even the rocks get a quick brooming. When the plants are in flower be careful in your movements so that you don't disturb the blossoms.

There are some other finishing details that can be attended to now. Leaves can be arranged to cover rocks or spread out evenly over soil without fear of future disturbance, no wind being present. Soil can be poked and shaped around rocks, so that the rocks seem to grow out of the soil rather than just being placed on top. Hollow soil out under a shelving rock to form a shadow.

Try to avoid a straight-across or a straight-down line where the soil meets the glass. Break the line into terraces and hollows, sculpting the landscape as you go along.

This is an exciting time of small refinements that develop the subtleties of the view and make the landscape real—creating your own little world.

Cleaning the inside of the glass.

Cleaning the Glass

With the long spout of the watering can just touching the glass, dribble lukewarm water slowly along the inside of the panes to clean away any dust accumulated during the planting. Don't use a drop more than you have to, but make sure that every surface is flushed. This added moisture is all the terrarium still needs to function perfectly.

Now wipe the outside of the terrarium with a sponge dipped in a mild solution of ammonia or vinegar until it sparkles.

The Cover Glass

Unless the opening of a container is very narrow it is always advisable to have a cover of glass or plastic. For our terrarium we have had the local hardware store cut a sheet of windowpane glass to size. It is ½-inch wider and longer than the top of the terrarium, to permit handling and to prevent it from falling into the tank if

All the terrariums should have cover glasses although, for illustrative reasons, we have left most of them out. Usually we have the glass cut a bit larger than the opening so that it can be handled more easily. To prevent cuts have the edges ground down.

we angle it in adjusting the space we usually leave a little open.

The same general rule, of having the cover a little wider than the opening, should be followed when you are planting other vessels as terrariums. It is one of the faults of the dome type of terrarium that its opening is at the bottom, fitted into a receptacle, so that the space within is really sealed from the outside air. For a short period this is fine but in due time, in a modern home, heat and the slightest carelessness in watering will cause such containers to malfunction and the plants to rot out. Vessels with the opening at the top are always much safer.

Lighting the Terrarium

If our terrarium were planted exclusively with shade-loving foliage material we could place it near a window and depend on reflected light to keep the plants healthy. With flowering plants, if you live in the country, this light may even be sufficient but city growers will find it quite inadequate. Fluorescent light is always far more reliable with blooming plants.

We have set a 24-inch two-tube fixture with reflector over the cover glass of the terrarium. We know growers who have had success with the lights in this position. But it is certainly not ideal since the heat from the lamps is excessive and it is difficult to manipulate the cover glass which must be kept partly open most of the time. The fixture can be suspended a few inches above the top of the terrarium by attaching it to a shelving or to a stand of sufficient height.

A 24-inch, two-tube, 20-watt fluorescent fixture with reflector has been set on top of the cover glass. This is a normal commercial model. The plates at the ends facilitate hanging or attaching to an overhead surface. If you do not intend to do this, you can buy a fixture without this feature. The reflector is finished in white enamel but you can paint it a decorative color.

The terrarium in an unused fireplace.

The Terrarium Finds a Home

The terrarium fits neatly into our unused fireplace and is a far better solution to the use of this regrettable (we wish we had the real thing) feature of many old houses and apartments in large cities than any other. Our fluorescent fixture has been shoved up into the opening of the flue where it is secured by masonry screws. As it is suspended several inches (5) above the terrarium cover glass and the plants within, we can keep the cover closed during much of the year.

Mirror, mantelpiece, fireplace, and terrarium are now in an informal but attractive relationship to each other. The terrarium has become as much a permanent decoration of the room as the Japanese dragon, the Chinese jade ring, or the Italian ceramic decoy duck. In other words, it has become living furniture in our home.

The terrarium needs no more attention than our floors, carpets, and furniture, yet it is a constant *changing* delight. Some growth, budding, or flowering is going on all the time and we are watching a scene which is developing day by day. It will pass through phases of flowering followed by only leaf growth; we will have to clean up occasionally; and it will suddenly burst into patterns of amazing color, reaching its perfection without repeating itself in quite the same way each time. No other kind of growing in the home can compare.

The finished terrarium a few weeks later.

3 🌿

Caring for
Your Terrarium

Lighting for Terrariums

You can control rather easily everything that goes on inside a terrarium. But it is a costly fallacy to imagine that your newly acquired or planted garden can thrive anywhere in the house. Sufficient light to grow the plants is absolutely essential. In most instances you must install fluorescent lights in order to keep the plants growing and blooming. None of the manufacturers of terrariums or kits give specific instructions on this point (Raja Toy Company—see listings —"proves" the rule), and most failures are due to ignorance on this subject.

Woodland Plant Terrariums

All of the plants in these terrariums grow in shade on the woodland floor. Nevertheless, during the shorter days of winter, the season when these gardens are most popular, they are placed on the windowsill either in direct or strong reflected light. The preferred planter has always been a round glass bowl or snifter with a large opening which is never covered. Principally because of the greater temperature drop at night in the country, as compared with a home in city or suburb, they generally flourish best in farmhouses. An additional reason, however, is that smog cuts the light in urban areas.

If you want to have them away from a window these terrariums must be lighted by either a Circline or a one-tube, 20-watt straight fluorescent lamp. Either of these will supply sufficient light at a distance of 12 inches on a 12-to-14-hour cycle. Woodland plants will not do well under incandescent bulbs because of the heat. All these plants prefer it rather cool, especially at their roots.

Tropical Foliage Plants

Virtually all the foliage plants we use are tolerant of shade. In the modern terrarium transparent covers are sometimes used, sometimes not. This partly depends on the size of the opening—a small one often not requiring a cover. With cover, the plants need less attention because of the smaller amount of evaporation. But you must be careful not to drown the plants with an excess of water and to see that the container does not become overheated. For this last reason a sunny windowsill is a rather precarious place, as a sunny day can "cook" the plants. A position in reflected or diffused light, back from or to the side of a window, is safer.

With fluorescent light it is possible to have your terrarium anywhere in the house. Short round bowls can be kept under Circline lamps—the standard kitchen fixture kind will do. Fish tanks do best under a 20-watt 24-inch fluorescent lamp with reflector. The latter can be suspended from any shelf surface or an appropriately high stand which you have bought or made. Use one Warm White and one Cool White lamp in the fixture. Set it 6 to 15 inches over the top of the terrarium and leave it on about 14 hours daily. If the lamp is too far away you will notice that the plants elongate. If it is too close the leaves may turn brown at the tips. And if the placement is just right the plants will remain compact and grow slowly with short internodes.

Foliage terrariums (and bottle gardens) can also be lighted by spots or floods. The best of these for the purpose is the G.E. Cool Beam which is available in a number of wattages with narrow, medium, and wide beams. Special fixtures are required for these lamps but they will not scorch the plants. The terrarium must receive at least 150 footcandles illumination. A 300-watt flood attached to an 8-foot ceiling will adequately light a foliage terrarium on a 36-inch table.

Flowering Plants

Optimum conditions must be provided in order to get plants to flower—even those select ones which we recommend. A minimum of 400 footcandles is required to bloom even African Violets. Providing intense light also raises temperatures, and these plants will not tolerate over 85° inside the terrarium for very long.

As we have noted, the flowering plants will do best with a cover glass. But if we are to have the lights close to the plants we must also take measures to prevent overheating. This is the reason why we cannot use incandescent lamps. It also means that we must open the terrarium, by shoving the cover aside, whenever room temperatures climb. This is because the heat of the lamps is constant. In a cool room this heat may be actually helpful in keeping temperatures over the 60° minimum. But the moment temperatures rise outside, the heat from the lamps can be damaging. Air-conditioned rooms, therefore, are best.

Because of their relative coolness we use fluorescent tubes. Unless the terrarium is small, Circline fluorescent lamps may be inadequate to produce bloom. A double fixture (one ring inside the other) will work better. A single large plant is about all they can serve, for they are considerably less efficient than straight tubes. A two-tube, 20-watt fluorescent fixture with reflector, using Warm White and Cool White lamps in combination on a sixteen-hour cycle, and placed 3 to 4 inches over the terrarium, will produce good bloom. Standing the lamp right on top of the cover glass is effective but inhibits handling and can be too hot.

A problem, which can be handled only by experiment and juggling, is that some of the plants may be high and others low in your arrangement—therefore nearer to or farther from the lights. The solution is to plant the less light-demanding ones low and the others higher.

The lighting of blooming terrariums with spots and floods has not been solved as yet. The use of mirror on the back wall of a terrarium will increase its efficiency considerably.

Cactus and Succulent Terrariums

These plants are accustomed to such intense light that you should not start out with the idea that you are going to have bloom. The state of light technology does not permit that in most cases. Furthermore, quite a large percentage of these plants will bloom only after a change in day length corresponding to the change in the seasons. You should rather consider these arrangements as a sort of living sculpture and concentrate on preserving the good appearance of the plants. If there is insufficient light they will not only fail to bloom but will etiolate—a word that describes the ugly thin growth that takes place when succulents make a desperate effort to reach the light.

You will get your best results with maximum light. In the country the terrarium can be placed on the windowsill with the cover on. So little moisture will be inside that the danger of burn is small. In the city a windowsill is inadequate and maximum artificial light must be used.

We would certainly recommend, at least for tanks and other larger terrariums, use of three or, preferably, four fluorescent tubes with reflector placed directly over the terrarium. Since the cover needs only a rare moving this is no great inconvenience. The tubes should be alternating Warm White and Cool White, 20 watts. Keep the lights on sixteen to eighteen hours per day.

With these provisions you may get bloom on some of your plants, for instance, Rebutias, Anacampseros, Haworthias, and Stapelias. If you want to experiment with seasonal light changes you will have to use an astronomical timer that will change the day length automatically to conform with seasonal sunrise and sunset.

Fluorescent Light

We would not be discouraging regarding daylight if we did not have a much better alternative. Fluorescent light, the coolest and most efficient form of illumination, will guarantee you "sunny" days for your terrarium every day without fail all year round. The results with artificial light are far superior to dependence on natural light.

Foliage terrariums with low light requirements usually will perform quite well under the ceiling fluorescents of a modern office building. The seven or eight hours of illumination is quite sufficient.

In the home it is advisable to use a fluorescent fixture attached either to the bottom of a shelf or to a stand, so that it is situated a few inches above the cover glass. The fixtures are made with straight tubes and Circline lamps. Although less efficient the Circlines can be made into attractive stands overhanging circular terrariums. The best fixtures of the straight type have two tubes and come in a number of lengths related to their wattages. For a 24-inch terrarium such as we have been describing a two-tube, 20-watt, 24-to-25-inch fixture is best for foliage or flowering plants. If the surface from which the fixture is suspended is painted flat white a separate reflector may be unnecessary. Otherwise it is advisable, and commercial fixtures in a number of different lengths are available with reflectors.

You can also purchase prefab tabletop fluorescent fixtures which consist of the fixture and reflector with stands at either end. If the stands permit raising and lowering of the reflector to the required height over your particular terrarium they are an easy solution. Most of these fixtures are unattractively finished but can be made quite sightly by enameling them on the outside in a decorator color or to match your wall.

The best way is to make a stand yourself. It is quite simple to construct a lightweight sawhorse, for instance, and suspend the fixture from it by hooks or chains. Simple rigid posts at either end can be designed and built in any number of ways, and in all sizes.

The fluorescent tubes recommended by the Indoor Light Gardening Society of America are a combination (one of each) of tubes designated Warm White and Cool White or Daylight; or Gro-Lux Wide Spectrum and Cool White. These are normal commercial tubes such as are used for institutional and business lighting, except for the Gro-Lux which is a "growth" tube at a reasonable price. These lamps can be bought in hardware or department stores or electrical shops.

Although they are less efficient for growth, floodlights can be used, situated on the ceiling of a room or angled from ceiling poles or the walls. Best of the floods for the purpose are the G.E. Cool Beam Floods, which come in a number of wattages. These lamps are provided with a glass filter that removes the hot rays which would damage your plants through overheating of the terrarium. Ceramic sockets must be used, and these floods are usually set in bullet fixtures. Since a good deal of interior lighting is now done with floods reflecting from walls, instead of table lamps and ceiling reflectors, the use of the Cool Beam will fit in well with modern schemes of lighting.

Incandescent lamps placed close enough to a terrarium to cause growth emit too much heat to be practical.

Watering

Maintaining an approximately correct moisture level in a terrarium is far easier when the plants are in pots. When different kinds with varying moisture requirements are planted directly in the soil, the moisture level of the terrarium must always conform to the needs of the plant that needs the most water. This usually means that the terrarium becomes waterlogged in short order. The plants that do not require constant moisture either grow excessively fast or succumb to the excess. In any event it is altogether impossible to regulate the moisture and humidity so that a satisfactory recycling can take place.

With the plants in pots there is one disadvantage. According to their rate of consumption, some plants will absorb the water in the soil of the pots more rapidly than others. The only way to check the condition of the pots is by poking a finger into the soil of each one. This should be done once a week in summer and usually every two weeks in winter. Assuming that you have not jammed your terrarium with plants, this is no great chore. Otherwise pot planting in a terrarium is much superior.

Water with a narrow-spouted can and take care of each pot individually according to its needs. In the basic terrarium we have just built, the *Begonia* and the *Episcia* should be kept just barely moist while the *Gesneria* prefers to be very wet at all times. As for the *Sinningia pusilla* which are in foundation soil, they can have a few teaspoons of water dribbled in their immediate neighborhood. The fern must be moist.

Do not overwater and do not, above all, pour in so much that some ends up in the drainage below. That should, ideally, remain dry.

It is obvious that ultimately, with our cover open part of the time (see Ventilation), the foundation soil will become completely dried out. This is not desirable because it will absorb both the moisture from the pots and the humidity from the air. The grains of perlite and peat moss will stick together when the soil is just moist. When dry, the particles will be separate and the color of the mix appear lighter. Another indication is when the glass stops frosting at night, as it should if the moisture is sufficient.

When the foundation mix has become too dry, water can be poured along the inside of the glass. Do not pour into the center, for you will simply wash soil away from mounds and rocks. In a large terrarium it is impossible to water evenly. But if a sufficient amount is added to the tank it will spread through the mix evenly within twenty-four hours. On the whole it is best to water in small amounts over a period of days until, by the frosting of the glass at night, you will know that the terrarium is in balance.

It is also useful to know the signs of overwatering. Even a properly balanced terrarium will steam and accumulate large drops on its cover pane if the temperature within the container is excessive or if the temperature drops suddenly. All indications of overwatering therefore are to be judged in terms of the behavior of your terrarium when the temperature is in the range between 65° and 75° Fahrenheit.

When a terrarium is properly balanced and the cover is on, the glass should fog up but without accumulating large drops. When the temperature drops at night, water of condensation will gather on the inside of the panes and the fogging may be heavier. However, it should clear up shortly after the lights are turned on in the morning. A light hazing is not a harmful sign.

When you have overwatered the signs will be evident, not only on the panes, but will be observable in the behavior of the plants.

If there is water in the drainage the cover glass will accumulate enough moisture to drip, and within twenty-four to forty-eight hours, with a closed cover glass, the plants will start to show areas of black rot on their leaves or a gray webbing will start to grow over the ground and onto the plants. This is deadly and may happen so fast that you will be unable to halt it.

As soon as you note the slightest appearance of overwatering, remove the cover glass and allow the soil to dry out until it is just moist. With the cover off you can check this by feel. If you fear that your individual pots will dry out too much in the process they can be tested and lightly watered, if needed, without changing the moisture level of the terrarium as a whole.

Temperature

The ideal temperature range is 65° to 75° Fahrenheit *inside the terrarium*. Temperatures up to 85° are tolerated. Beyond that, watch out. On dog days in August, if you are not favored with air conditioning, take the cover glass off completely and, in the bargain, set a fan to cooling the terrarium. The natural humidity at that time is high enough for the plants.

Temperatures below 65° Fahrenheit inhibit bloom in most of our tropical plants. A striking exception is certain orchids which tolerate a coolness of 55° or even less. Don't expect to have a successfully blooming terrarium unless temperatures are maintained within the ranges indicated. When the thermometer drops below 65° there is as much danger of fungal rot, in the presence of excess moisture in the terrarium, as if the temperature were 30° higher. Keep your terrarium relatively dryer in both hot and cold spells.

Most foliage and blooming plants do not require a sharp drop in temperature at night to provide the dew of condensation to the plants. The prevalent high humidity day and night is all they need to stay fresh and vigorous. There is always some drop in temperature after sundown or the lights are turned off.

Ventilation

The whole idea of a terrarium is contrary to the theory that all plants need ventilation. For some reason plants in a greenhouse or on a windowsill depend on moving air. And the anomaly is that these same plants bask in the terrarium stuffiness.

As we have indicated our greatest dangers are overwatering and overheating. To counteract these requires a certain amount of skill in handling the cover glass. On coolish days we keep the cover on tight to keep warmth in. On warmer days we open up the cover about an inch. And on hot, humid days we may remove it entirely.

Fertilizer

Because the plants in a terrarium enjoy such an ideal microclimate, they need less fertilizer than when grown in the open room. Another consideration, of course, is that we have no desire to see these plants grow quickly. Starve them a bit and they will remain compact and will bloom just as well. Tiny quantities of fertilizer work more efficiently in a terrarium because they remain in the soil and are not leached out with plain water as happens in the ordinary windowsill or light garden. For the same reason too much fertilizer soon accumulates a residue that becomes dangerous to plants.

We almost never fertilize our terrarium plants. Once every three months is certainly ample and in a dosage no different from what is normally given to plants a few times a month or with every watering. One tenth the strength recommended by the manufacturer of the fertilizer is quite sufficient.

For foliage plants we recommend a balanced formula known as 20-20-20, representing 20 percent each nitrate, phosphate, and potash. For the blooming plants low nitrate and high phosphate and potash is best.

Pests

There are no problems of pests in terrariums—or there are nothing *but* problems. By this we mean that the terrarium should, as far as insects are concerned, be sterile. The enclosure of the garden means that it is most unlikely that insects will get in.

But a terrarium is no place to put a plant that is harboring insects. Once inside they run rampant and all your plants are immediately affected. That is the end of your planting. Remove the plants and the soil and wash out the container with a strong solution of Clorox. After a few days you can begin all over again.

Since your soil is sterile, only an infected plant can cause real trouble. Any plants purchased from florist or nursery, or acquired recently, should be quarantined for at least two weeks prior to planting in the terrarium.

Plants removed from a terrarium because of pests need not be discarded. Keep them apart from other plants; treat them for the pests involved, and they can live on happily ever after—even return to a terrarium existence.

Keeping the Terrarium Clean

The high humidity in the terrarium breeds algae, whose spores are present in the air. A green scum forms on the lower part of the panes, where they contact the soil, and spreads into colonies of green muck, sometimes invading the moister areas around pots and plants. Protection against algae is another reason for using pots. Not that algae can do very much damage but the effect is unsightly. The moister the terrarium, the more algae will accumulate with time.

Wiping the panes with a moist cloth will remove most of the scum. But growths in soil have to be treated. Tropical fish stores sell algicide pills with which you can make a solution and spray the inside of the terrarium, panes and plants, without damage. A solution of one teaspoon of Clorox to a gallon of water is also said to be helpful. Of course the amount of water you will use is very small. A spray is better than a drench.

Otherwise our only advice is to keep the terrarium as gleaming clean as possible so that your arrangements will look their best.

Trimming and Grooming Plants

Controlling the spread of the plants perpetuates the ideal appearance of your terrarium. After it is ready it often takes anywhere from several days to weeks for it to reach the peak of perfection, as plants recover from handling and change of environment and grow sufficiently to fill part of their extra allotted spaces. From there on it is a battle to keep them in condition and from crowding each other out. Pots help to control them. But some trimming is often necessary.

We say this is necessary but there are plenty of growers who will display with pride a terrarium which is a mass of tangled foliage. They apparently see beauty in sheer vigor. We do not. The extra trouble, in our opinion, is worthwhile because any arrangement should preserve a semblance of order and chaos is not art.

You can't trim every plant. Single-stemmed ones are impossible because they only grow in one direction—up. When they have outgrown the terrarium they must be removed. Dracaenas and members of the Arum family are of this type. Similarly, stemless and rosette plants can't be cut down. The most we can do is remove extra leaves, which is usually not harmful to the plant (outside leaves only, please). If more than one rosette appears the oldest and most unsightly one can be removed. Your greatest satisfaction will be in trimming branching plants such as Begonias. Do not be afraid to do it ruthlessly. Just cut any branch that doesn't look right. Trimming will actually improve the growth habit of the plant. The cuttings can be rooted, potted, and given to your friends. Within a week or two such plants no longer bear evidence of this surgery.

Grooming takes many forms—removing dead or rotten leaves, cutting the pedicels of flowers that have bloomed, building up soil that has compacted, resetting stones that have worked themselves loose, cleaning pebbles and rocks so that they gleam again, and so forth. This is housekeeping with plants. If you enjoy your terrarium you will be happy keeping it in shape.

Changing Plants

No plant lasts forever and therefore the same goes for terrarium plantings. Dr. Ward may have kept a terrarium going for fifteen years, but we'll bet it was a hideous mess most of the time. Actually a terrarium which just goes on and on becomes a bad habit and a bore. Even a cactus garden should get going and do something after a while.

Our more active plants all have their youth, prime, and old age within a period of a year or two. They either outgrow their spaces or become woody or potbound. Whatever the details they eventually reach the point where they are no longer an ornament. At this point they have to be replaced.

Lifting out the pot should be done gingerly, to disturb the surrounding soil and rocks as little as possible. Have a new plant—not necessarily the same kind—ready to set in its place. That is all there is to it except some cleaning up of any disturbance. In this way all your plants will gradually be replaced with a consequent change in the appearance of the terrarium garden. If you have chosen your new plants with good taste they will provide combinations of form and color which are as good as or better than the first planting.

Plants removed from terrariums should be hardened off for a week or two. Place them in plastic bags which are slightly open, increasing the ventilation every few days until they become adjusted to the lower humidities and temperature irregularities of your living and gardening area.

Occasionally, by accident rather than design, a plant will spread and take over a large part of a terrarium in such a way that it gives satisfaction rather than becomes a nuisance. A terrarium we made for a friend contained a fine-leaved Boston fern which soon spread right across the bottom. But the growth was so feathery and soft and spectacular—the most beautiful we have ever seen—that it was allowed to run rampant and other plants which it covered with its leaves were taken out. That, however, happens once in a lifetime.

4 🌿

Other
Terrarium Plantings

A Cactus and Succulent Terrarium

Cactus and succulent dish gardens are common in florist shops. And they are popular with both the florist and his customers because, compared to other kinds of plants, they need little attention for long stretches of time. Usually they get none at all while in the shop and, if totally neglected by their new owner, will still survive for many months. Of course they will eventually die of thirst if not watered at all, and of rot if they are watered incautiously. The longer a succulent is without water the more careful you must be in providing its first drinks—a rule which applies as well to humans rescued in the desert.

People who know succulents are horrified at the way these are planted commercially. Because the dishes are shallow, the plants are set in a combination of clay and sand which has the solidity of concrete. Under the best of care they will not thrive in such a medium. To save them you must dig them up and replant them in better soil.

Since cacti and succulents require little water and humidity, properly planted dish gardens will do. So the question arises: Why plant them in terrariums? One reason is that the framing seems to enhance their appearance. Another, that though the terrarium is kept relatively dry, these plants do benefit from the inevitable humidity in the closed tank. In the desert that is what they live on most of the time. At night it congeals in the form of dew. In fact their thick leaves or obese stems, not only serve for water storage but heat storage. As temperature decreases with extreme speed in the desert as soon as the sun sets, the leaf or stem, which is still warm, immediately attracts any slight moisture in the air, and the plant absorbs it throughout the night.

Growing cacti and succulents in the house is a difficult matter. Unless they receive sufficient light they will etiolate—develop those thin long growths which are so ugly. Of course, in the country right on the windowsill in full sun they will do all right. In the city it is hopeless without artificial means. In a terrarium, with a fluorescent light set directly above and aided by the internal humidity of the tank, they grow well if watered with great care.

We have always considered the tropical fish tank, or large plastic or glass globes with covers, to be ideal for making desert pictures which are far more attractive than the productions of the commercial florists. Furthermore, since we plant in pots, the arrangement can be changed at will—even more easily than with green plants. A well-arranged cactus and succulent terrarium has great beauty and requires minimum care.

It seems that every time we start a square terrarium our first move is to put something in the corner. We couldn't see a hill in this one with a cactus sitting on top. But we wanted height somewhere. This big piece of slag, looking like lava rock, attracted our attention so we set it upright.

The other large stones were placed with the idea of some terracing behind them and also that, by breaking the terrarium down the middle they would give the effect of depth, as in the dark, light, dark horizontals in landscape paintings. Also we had a couple of plants we thought would look well peeking out behind them.

Here is our tentative placement of the plants. The soil under the corner stone has been built up, raising it an inch or two. Our tallest plant is a *Graptopetalum,* so we put that in the left corner. And a fine cluster of golden spiny cacti is behind the rock on the right. Two other plants are placed tentatively. The white stone on the right was removed later.

If you haven't a true sand to cover your foundation mix, you can use perlite instead. Our picture shows approximately how this would look, except that the pots are not yet hidden. The pure white material does not bring out the color of the plants as well but it provides reflection which is good for them. A few stones have been added in the center and begin to hide the pot behind them. There are an additional haworthia and an aloe.

More plants are added and the pots are partly buried. The last photo showed clearly that the *Graptopetalum* would be partially obscured and somewhat downgraded by the bumpy cactus in front of it. It has therefore been raised up by fill-in with foundation mix and taken out of the vertical by tilting forward.

A hybrid Japanese grafted cactus has been placed behind the stone on the left partly hiding the less attractive lower part. The graft is the familiar orange one of the shops (*Gymnocalycium mihanovichii,* some mouthful). Smaller plants have been added up front. *Crassula lycopodioides,* the Club Moss Crassula, looks like a small succulent tree growing against the big rock.

The left side of the finished terrarium. We scraped up some surface, light-colored sand in the Pine Barrens of New Jersey. This is our topdressing. It is grainy yet not too coarse, and it has enough pine needles and twigs in it to be more lifelike.

Smaller stones have been added. Note the ones on the left in the corner so that the plant seems to be in a depression and the leaves are set off against them. White pebbles now completely surround the cactus cluster, and a matching piece of limestone replaces the darker piece which was in front of it. The shell fills an empty space where another cactus would look redundant.

The sand has been carefully molded and swept so that rocks overhang and so that it is visible between them. The cacti do not stick out but seem to grow out of it.

Detail of the right side of the finished terrarium. Plants and masses have been carefully proportioned.

The finished terrarium. Certainly this is not at all the usual bowl or tank with plants indiscriminately set in it. You will have no difficulty doing other equally handsome and lasting arrangements.

Medium for the Plants

As with other houseplants, our own mix for succulents is usually better than that supplied by a nursery. If possible your plants should be repotted in the following mix:

>1 part peat moss
>2 parts perlite
>1 part vermiculite
>¼ part limestone chips (optional)

We always use the limestone but there are good cactus growers who consider it unnecessary. If you use powdered horticultural lime, cut the proportion in half again. Add 1 cup of water to moisten.

If you can get good gritty sand (sterilized) you may prefer the following mix:

>1 part peat moss
>2 parts gritty sand
>1 part perlite
>¼ part limestone chips (optional)

Whereas regular houseplant mix should be packed lightly but firmly around plants, cacti and succulents require that it be tamped down. Otherwise they will wobble in the dry medium. As this mix is much more porous than commercial ones you run no danger of overhardening it.

Pots for these plants should be the smallest possible—4 inches at most. Desert plants do not like overpotting. In most cases 1½ to 2 inches is plenty. Plastic pots are best.

For the planting of our cactus garden we are using the same size tank as for our flowering and foliage garden.

The Foundation

Most cactus gardens are the same soil all the way through. If it is hard, the plants won't thrive. If it is pure sand the plants will be insecure. Even the sandy mix we have given as an alternative has the disadvantage of being very heavy; and we like our terrariums to weigh less than a ton so that we can move them around at will. Also sand is rather shifty for holding pots and stones in place. So, what we use is the peat mix without sand for the foundation as well as the pots. For cacti we build up with nearly dry medium. We also supply no separate drainage as it is entirely unnecessary.

Planning

We find that we handle cacti and succulents rather differently from flowering and foliage plants. The former are so slow growing that our arrangement can be considered as a static one and the individual plants as sculptures. The combination of rocks and plants becomes even more important. And we choose plants not for their blooming or foliage but purely on their fitting into the design as static elements. Among the cacti and succulents we are not limited, as we are among the others, by adaptability to the terrarium environment. Therefore we pick out our plants not according to their cultural characteristics at all but simply on appearance—size, texture, shape. Except for the specialist a cactus-succulent garden is anonymous.

Also we do not have to consider growth potential. We set the plants where they look best. And we are not so concerned with sculpturing the foundation as in causing the rocks to vie with the cacti for attention. Often a more level arrangement is best with the rocks and plants creating the high and low points.

5

Other
Terrarium Containers

The following pages contain photographs of the products of various glass and plastics manufacturers and distributors. They will give some idea of the wealth of forms suitable for terrariums which can be bought in department stores, gift shops, and other outlets all over the country.

Plastic Terrariums

We consider plastic terrariums inferior to glass in almost every respect except weight. Among our hobbies, working with plastic is not included. So we can speak of this material only from our experience of terrariums made with it.

It is our impression that square Lucite terrariums made of bonded sheets are best. But they must be perfectly cut, bonded, and polished. Of all the containers of plastic that we have used these seem most resistant to the action of soil chemicals. Such terrariums are, however, size for size, much more expensive than glass.

We guess that most commercial plastic terrariums, miniature

greenhouses, and so on, are made of inferior plastics which are often slightly tinted and which invariably become scratched. The action of moist soil soon clouds the surface. Cleaning is then impossible.

On the whole we can recommend plastic only for temporary use —glass is that much superior.

Terrarium Shapes

Except for some of the plastic greenhouses and bubbles and the Riekes-Crisa glass, we have seen hardly any designs specially manufactured for terrarium use that are properly proportioned for arranging or growing plants. Often too little space is provided at the bottom for soil. There is usually insufficient room for foliage to spread and, where width is provided, the terrariums are too low. No matter how small the plants, they seem to be crowded in these containers from the start. Many are only useful for single pot plants of a specific shape—provided you have them or can get them.

Florists get around these problems by using very low, slow-growing plant material or selling you the idea that their foliage plants won't continue to spread—which they invariably do.

Glass Terrariums

We have listed separately the manufacturers of terrariums among which you will find those made of glass. The material is durable, brilliant, transparent, and easy to maintain. It can be replanted time and again without damage. Even the most artistic glass can be used for the purpose.

Hemisform I, made by Dome Enterprises and sold through the Kenton Collection as The Aqua Dome, is a 40-gallon plastic bowl with base. The cover is of glass. Expensive and beautiful, this is the queen of terrarium containers. Any terrarium buff can make a handsome garden in this supertank.

The acme of terrarium elegance. The dining table has a 42 x 72-inch top of ¾-inch glass. The frame is of highly polished chrome and stands 28 inches high. A Plexiglas bowl ¼ inch thick and 11 inches deep holds the terrarium. Dome Enterprises, Inc., Dallas, Texas.

Square end table, glass-topped, with Plexiglas bowl. Dome Enterprises, Inc.
Parsons tables of wood can be used for the same purpose.

Hemisform II, an original design by Dome Enterprises. The tables are planned to hold one or two terrariums.

Hemisform III in the 3-foot-high model is the largest of its kind. What are we to say of the 5-foot model which is also available? A monster—better suited to an institution than a home. But what a magnificent piece of natural furniture—if you have the space.

Designed by John H. Nickerson, Jr., for Blenko Glass Company, this classic hand-blown vase with cover makes a superb home for terrarium plantings.

A 20- — yes, 20 — inch vase from Blenko which offers infinite possibilities. Here craft and horticulture can combine forces to make a thing of beauty.

Plastic bubble on ring stand by Lucidity. The stand is separate so that you can angle your garden as you please.

Glass and metal terrariums by B.L. Designs.

The centerpiece is a two-part plastic terrarium by Aldermaston Sales. The top is clear, the bottom a bright opaque color. The glass on the left is a typical apothecary or herb jar. The two pieces on the right are simple glass containers from variety stores. Jinny has glued on, with cement, three plastic dry cleaners' clips, shaped like bobby pins. The one part will now fit on the other without jiggling. Eureka—a terrarium.

Hand-blown Glass Terrariums

Among the glass manufacturers the greatest variety of forms for terrarium use is produced by Riekes-Crisa, hand-blown in Mexico. An important part of their business is terrariums, and a number of the models have been specially designed for the purpose. This is the only company we know that provides glass lids for their brandy snifters and bubbles, saving you the necessity of having a cover glass made to order. The following illustrations are excellent examples of shapes to look for when planning a decorative terrarium.

We have used some of this glass for our own terrariums and photos. This set is from the manufacturer and the plants—alas—are of plastic.

Really a bubble on its own stand, brandy snifters have long been popular for terrariums. Riekes-Crisa makes them in ten sizes from small 12-ounce to a huge 820-ounce size—with lids.

Riekes-Crisa calls this its "modern terrarium."

Handsome candy jars—or terrariums—by Riekes-Crisa.

A hanging bubble. One way to enjoy a terrarium. Macramé hangers are even better looking.

With these great vessels, which come in three sizes, you can make barrel terrariums.

A shapely low bubble. Riekes-Crisa makes a round one in eight sizes up to a whopping 16 inches in diameter.

The large terrarium.

Large terrarium with corner "beach." The blooming plant is *Crosandra undulaefolia*. In the corner is *Gesneria pedicellaris x citrina* (yellow). *Chirita sinensis*, and the Boston fern, *Nephrolepsis* 'Norwood,' complete the arrangement.

Terrarium with a head-on design. This terrarium was planned to be seen from at least two sides. The big rock acts as the transitional element between low and high land. *Streptocarpus* 'Mini-Nymph' is the central plant. In the right corner is *Sinningia pusilla* and next to it is *Chinaea multiflora. Pilea depressa* cascades downward and *xGloxinera* 'Pink Petites' line the horizon.

Terrarium without foundation soil: *Biophytum sensitivum, Gesneria cuneifolia,* and *Oxalis martiana aureo-reticulata.*

Terrarium without foundation soil: *Portulacaria afra-variegata* ar *Sinningia* 'Cindy.'

A *Seemannia latifolia* in full bloom with only a fern for a companion. The "beach" is at the left and the rest of the landscape simply contributes to the display of this magnificent plant.

Handsome Blenko vase with African Violet "Lisa" and young plants of *Oxalis martiana aureoreticulata.*

A snifter as sphagnum moss terrarium. The yellow flowers belong to the rare and beautiful *Begonia prismatocarpa. Sinningia* 'Freckles' is behind it and *S.* 'White Sprite' in front. These are among the most floriferous of houseplants.

A terrarium planting without soil in the large tank. *Oncidium ornithorhynchum,* an orchid, has four sprays of blossoms. On the left is an Aloe, and two plants of *Malpighia coccigera* are on the right. Here the rocks are almost as important as the plants, whose pots are completely hidden.

Dracaena sanderiana in the large Blenko vase. The others are *Saxifraga sarmentosa tricolor,* and *Pteris cretica albo-lineata.*

This Pyrex vessel by Corning is 24 inch high. *Begonia* 'Sachsen,' *Hypoestes so guinolenta,* partly hidden on the rig *Serissa foetida,* and *Asparagus plumos on the left.*

A great Blenko vase planted with *Ge neria pedicellaris x citrina, Columne* 'Chanticleer,' and *Sinningia* 'Doll Bab

Pyrex jar, 24 inches high, contains *Dracaena* by Doll,' *Begonia* 'Cleopatra,' and *Serissa* tida.

It takes a vessel as tall as this Pyrex jar to house our tall *Jacobinia carnea*. *Episcia* 'Cleopatra,' *Pilea* 'Moon Valley,' and *Episcia* 'Fanny Haage' nestle at its feet.

Jacobinia carnea spreads its wings in a 16-inch-diameter Pyrex jar. *Pteris gautheri* on the left. *Malpighia coccigera* on the right.

A foliage planting. Clockwise starting with the Prayer Plant in the center: *Sinningia schiffneri,* Coleus, *Serissa foetida, Asparagus plumosus.*

This is the largest of the Riekes-Crisa glass bubbles—16 inches in diameter. In the center is *Episcia* 'Jinny Elbert' accompanied by a *Fittonia* and a *Kohleria.* The design is symmetrical and concentric. We particularly like this one.

The Dwarf Pomegranate. Left, *Begonia masoniana.* Right, *Serissa foetida.* Large Pyrex jar by Corning.

This Riekes-Crisa 5-gallon jug has a convenient hole in the top. It is planted with an assortment of greenery.

The Pyrex (Corning) jar containing two plants of *Streptocarpus* 'Mini-Nymph' and a *Lantana nana compacta*. This is a combination which will be in continuous bloom.

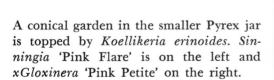

A conical garden in the smaller Pyrex jar is topped by *Koellikeria erinoides*. *Sinningia* 'Pink Flare' is on the left and x*Gloxinera* 'Pink Petite' on the right.

Mrs. Rosalia Rau's clever bromeliad terrarium in a B.L. Designs dome.

Aldermaston's original two-part plastic terrarium is planted with a single African Violet.

Succulent garden in Lucidity's plastic bubble. The cover is off so that the garden's picture can be taken.

A 5-gallon jug on its side is supported on a cradle. Riekes-Crisa has obligingly cut a hole in the side for easy terrarium planting. See our color illustration.

Still More Terrariums

These plastic bubbles by Christen are very well crafted and are available in many stores across the nation. This is one of the most popular small terrariums.

Hanging plastic bubbles by Christen.

Elegant Stolzle vases from Bonniers show types of glassware which make good terrariums (except the ashtrays, of course).

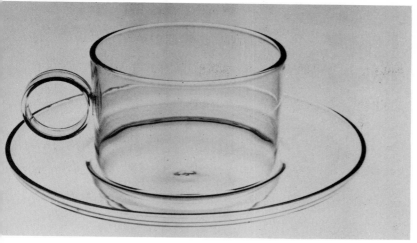

Steuben's "Creative Glass" has inspired many terrarium buffs. Even a tea (or coffee) cup like this one is an elegant frame around a garden of miniature plants (or a single).

The terrarium can be in the top or bottom.

Use the tall beaker or two of the small pots supported by plastic clips as in photograph on page 68.

In order to display it better (or bring it closer to fluorescent lights in a decorative way), have your terrarium in the top section and fit two or three of the matching sections below it.

A handsome taller pot in the "Creative Design" line by Steuben.

For cheese perhaps—but could be a handsome terrarium.

Something different in plastic by Gould Products. Available in variety stores. The shape is a particularly good one. Plants spread at the top.

Plastic goblet by **Gould Products.**

Greenhouse Kits

There are numerous kinds and sizes of indoor plastic greenhouses on the market. These are useful for raising plants from seeds but also make very good terrariums. The Raja Toy Company has an outstanding line of well-designed units. Raja has a cultural instruction booklet and is one of the few terrarium companies offering fluorescent light units and gardening supplies.

The small unit shown is ventilated and contains a stand holding twelve little pots. If you want to use it as a terrarium just remove the innards. A smaller model is also available.

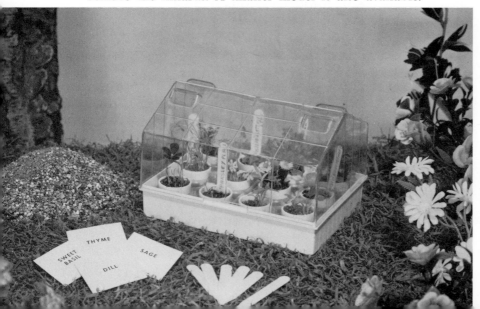

Raja's hi-rise model.

A larger indoor greenhouse with fluorescent fixture cleverly fitted onto the roof.

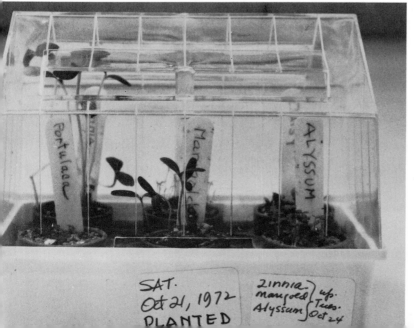

The Raja greenhouse is shown here with seedlings well up in the little pots. Terrarium conditions are maintained in these little units.

6

A Gallery of
Terrarium Plantings

In the following portfolio of pictures we have our own fun with the containers illustrated in the previous section, plus a number of others. We have used our own plants, just as presumably you will, so that the full gamut of plants which are suitable, listed in the next section, are by no means covered. What we have used are all the *types* of plants, so that you need only select similar plants, if you are interested in making similar designs.

All the designs are of the modern types. Those with foliage require only windowsill or reflected sunlight. Those with flowers, however, though possible in good natural light, do better under fluorescent fixtures. This free play of plants demonstrates the ease with which attractive long-lasting displays can be put together. And we hope it demonstrates how little the decorative effect depends on props, artificial figures, or other "realistic" details.

If we start off with set ideas of what terrariums should be we inevitably limit ourselves to certain sizes and shapes of containers. The advantage of the modern approach to terrarium planning is its flexibility. It is quite a liberation to be able to avail ourselves of these marvelous modern glass shapes and a challenge to find, in each case, a viable and attractive solution. Nothing could therefore be further from our thoughts than to straitjacket the reader by suggesting that our terrariums are the only answers. On the contrary the whole demonstration is for the purpose of setting you thinking about the possibilities of glassware or plastic containers combined with your own plants in your own home. Once you have started to plan freely you will, indeed, have fun with terrariums.

This is only our small 5-gallon, all-glass terrarium but gives the effect of something quite larger. This is due to the extreme angling of the landscape. The intention was to arrange it so that it could be seen from the narrow end and at an angle. The low part, therefore, is at one end. The rise is created by the big rock which effects it rather abruptly. And though, from there on, the climb is gentle, at an angle it appears steep because the soil follows a somewhat different route.

On top is *Streptocarpus* 'Mini-Nymph,' accompanied by *Sinningia pusilla* and *Phinaea multiflora,* the white flower. The greenery of *Pilea depressa* wanders down the side of the rock. On the other side are x*Gloxinera* 'Pink Petites.' This terrarium will have bloom most of the time.

Plants and stones ready for last stages of building the narrow-end terrarium.

Frontal view of the terrarium.

Pteris cretica albo-lineata, the variegated table fern, *Adiantum macrophyllum,* the large leaf Maiden Hair fern, and *Fittonia verschaffeltii,* the red-veined Fittonia, are the plants in this appealing arrangement by Dimitri Markatos of New York.

Mr. Markatos himself assembles the glass panes and sets them on a marble slab. Stones, black Japanese pebbles, limestone chips, greened limestone are used. Slabs of cork bark form the principal architecture. Baccto potting soil has been used in the foundation over marble chips. A terrarium of this shape and size has innumerable uses.

The terrarium on a sideboard. T'ang ewer to the left, Chimu stirrup-spout jar to the right, and a Rousseau flower piece above.

There are three levels to this terrarium—the perlite and pebble base on the right, a low soil foundation to the left and the whole rear more or less on the same level, with the plants creating most of the changes in height.

The centerpiece is *Crossandra undulaefolia*—with very shining dark green leaves and brilliant orange flowers in the shape of a fan. They can be grown from cuttings under fluorescent light and will then bloom on much shorter stems than we ordinarily see in the nursery or flower shop. The cluster of flowers at the top lasts for weeks. When cut back it will branch and produce several flowering stems. A spectacular plant for a terrarium.

The plant on the left is equally remarkable. It is a very recent cross of *Gesneria pedicellaris* (red) and *Gesneria citrina* (yellow) made by Michael Kartuz of Wilmington, Mass. The flowers are inch-long tubes in deep clear yellow. It is enormously vigorous and often has over fifty buds on its stem lining up to bloom. Constant moisture is necessary to keep it in shape. Some of the flowers were knocked off in planting (they don't take to handling at all), and it will be a few days before this plant will look its best again.

Chirita sinensis has rather large, leathery leaves which are hairy and veined irregularly in green and pure silver. They are quilted too, so that the effect is of some unusual kind of stamped leather. Quite slow growing, it will form a magnificent rosette with time.

The fern, *Nephrolepis exaltata* 'Norwoodii,' is a very fleecy Boston Fern that requires high humidity and little light.

Our great vase, on loan from Blenko, holds *Gesneria pedicellaris x citrina* (which will soon be among the most popular of house plants), *Sinningia* 'Doll Baby,' and *Columnea* 'Chanticleer.' Chanticleer is the most compact and easiest to bloom of the current Columneas and will soon be covered with flowers. Notice how the curve of the plant, starting high on the left and trailing onto the foundation soil, imparts motion to the design.

This beautiful hand-blown glass vase designed by John H. Nickerson, Jr., and blown at Blenko Glass Works serves as the housing for a "miracle plant," African Violet 'Lisa.' Lisa, which comes from Fischer Nurseries, Linwood, New Jersey, is as near perfect as an African Violet plant can be. The pink flowers are intense in color and crisp in texture. They are borne erect in the center of the rosette of leaves. The leaves are flat and symmetrical. And the plant is always in bloom.

We do not often use only a single plant in our terrariums but this exception, it seems to us, is justified. Vase and plant are both champions and beautifully complement each other.

Set the vase near a window or under a fluorescent tube and you will have continuous bloom with a little care. The vase has a fitted top so that moisture remains constant. Occasionally you will have to reach in with scissors and snip off old blossoms. Each one, however, lasts a long time in this ideal environment. Haul out the cut flowers with a pair of tongs.

We have set Lisa on a foundation of mix dusted with perlite and tilted it forward so that it will look its best and do justice to the vase. The babies up front are *Oxalis martiana aureo-reticulata*. It is possible with such glassware to plant with a number of foliage plants but the shape is not well adapted to most flowering ones. A single fine plant like this one is a real ornament and so easy to do.

A *Dracaena sanderiana* looks windblown in this magnificent vase as its leaves bend against the glass and it is perhaps too large for the purpose. But it will grow slowly and will adapt itself nicely so that the arrangement will last for quite a while. It is accompanied by an Apple Leaf Croton, *Saxifraga sarmentosa tricolor,* an amusing color variation of the common Strawberry Geranium, and the fern *Pteris ensiformis victoriae.*

The Dracaena can easily be replaced after a while by a similar but smaller plant.

Having landscaped and "planted" our big Pyrex jar we have removed the plants again, without disturbing the rocks or the soil, so that we have left the skeleton of the arrangement behind.

The three plants are three forms of *Gesneria cuneifolia,* each with a somewhat different colored flower and foliage. As long as they are watered regularly they will bloom. Nothing else is needed therefore to have a continuously flowering terrarium. The plants are low and the pots are short.

We see that a carefully built wall of stones will hide the pots adequately and produce a scene of sorts. The soil does build up to the rear and hides the back of the pots. But, if necessary, we could have used rocks all the way around.

This terrarium is shown on the floor. It is broad enough (16 inches) to serve as the base for a coffee table. All it requires is a big square, oblong, or circle of plate glass covering it. It can be lighted by short, angled fluorescent fixtures cemented on to the glass cover. If this is too complicated place it under a Parsons Table which has ample space to attach a 15- to 24-inch fluorescent fixture.

The terrarium assembled.

If you have a terrarium big enough to hold a good-sized dwarf Pomegranate you can make an arrangement like this. Your tree will bloom constantly and develop fruits like the one on the ground. Hardly anything quite matches it, and it puts the effect of most foliage completely to shame. On the left is a *B. masoniana*, the Iron Cross Begonia, somewhat dwarfed by poor culture and starvation which keeps it in hand. This time our Serissa grows through the knothole of a piece of dried bark. We don't much like to use wood in our terrariums but this piece is very dry, very thin, and rather ornamental. So we made an exception. The perlite does a good job of pushing the scene back from the viewer, straightening out the line, and acting as a color contrast. It is altogether impossible to lay down rules for handling these materials but the eye will tell you what to do. Notice how the perlite rises slightly toward the front. Without your being aware of it, it gives an effect of continuity.

Looking like a giant pink bird *Jacobinia carnea* spreads its wings over peaks which look like Rio's sugarloaf (a little). The long leafy plant is *Hoya bella* and the fern is *Pteris* 'Gautheri.' With that beach it's a little like Tahiti too.

In these large terrariums we show both small and large collections in the same space. Crowding is not so much a matter of using a few more plants as a matter of choosing ones which overlap each other. If your plants will stay in place and are small they will still give an air of spaciousness. We also repeat some plants so that different ways of working with the same kinds are demonstrated.

Our big wide Pyrex jar now contains a number of plants yet they will not become crowded for quite a while. *Maranta leuconeura,* var. *kerchoviana,* is the Prayer Plant of the flower shops. *Sinningia schiffneri* is a more unusual plant. Closely related to the Gloxinia, it is quite upright in growth and has wonderfully glowing velvety leaves. With plenty of light it will produce white flowers. Coleus is one of the most colorful and easiest of foliage plants. Even when quite small, like this one, it makes a real splash. Asparagus Fern, *Asparagus plumosus,* must be trimmed back but is easy to control. *Serissa foetida,* which we use so often, is very slow growing and can be trained and kept that way. *Aralia fruticosa,* one of the Parsley Aralias, grows to a great size. But little potted cuttings are just ideal because of their strangely cut and folded leaves and slow growth. When trimmed regularly they have the habit of branching from the base and making an odd little thicket. The Maranta produces little violet flowers and the Coleus minty white or violet ones in a spike.

Rocks are liberally used in the back of the composition, while up front we have placed some pieces of dark blue, purple, and green slag from old limekilns in Connecticut.

This landscape gives a shrubby effect in spite of the *Gesneria cuneifolia* in the center. The two rocks emphasize its importance and the rest of the greenery circles around. The small-leaved plant on the right is *Begonia bartonea,* which has silly tiny pink flowers in great numbers. Two ferns, a Serissa and a Prayer Plant fill in the rest. The four stones are purposely rather alike in size and shape, carrying the eye comfortably around the composition.

Our *Biophytum sensitivum* is pushed a bit against the glass, spoiling its symmetry. But all its oddity is brought out in this way and we know that it will grow very slowly and just continue to flap its "wings" without damage. As for the new *Gesneria pedicellaris x citrina,* by the time someone has found a "common name" for it it will be smothered in yellow tube flowers. It is doing a brooding job over the big rock. I guess we are getting anthropomorphic here to make an exception, for the small plants at the base look like young 'uns out for a stroll, overseen by rather ill-matched parents.

The little ones are pink *gloxinera* 'Pink Petite' and that remarkable terrarium plant *Phinaea multiflora* which is now bearing one of its little white cups but soon will have more. *Phinaea* will seed itself too and will never become a nuisance. Keep covered for best bloom.

The idea here was to use a number of our miniatures all together in a moderate-size columnar glass vessel. It is a Pyrex laboratory vessel from Corning, measuring approximately 10½ inches high and 8½ inches in diameter.

If one has a large greenhouse and specializes in miniature plants, it is not at all difficult to have any number of specimens in bloom when you need them for a purpose—for instance, planting terrariums. It is a different matter when the number of plants growing in the house is limited. One of the reasons for this book is that we are showing what can be done by someone dependent entirely on plants raised in the home or apartment under artificial light. We demonstrate in this way, too, the quite remarkable repertory already available to the indoor grower due to the efficiency of fluorescent light.

In our own collection we always have plenty of plants for terrariums. But in order to display and photograph them in bloom a number must flower simultaneously and be in good enough condition to be handled. Thus our selections are limited and you will find others in our plant lists. However, our photographs are of real plants, really grown in city conditions. And it has not been possible to show all the possibilities, and all the wealth of material available, because we do always have to wait for the right moment. For our own needs in terrarium planting we can take plants not yet in flower, knowing that, within a short time, they will be in bloom. You can do the same.

Here we have a number of miniatures which take up little space and therefore can produce a great deal of variety in a relatively small con-. tainer. The effect of the structure is of a little Mont St. Michel, a rocky peak with little plants set all around, on a rather thick bed of foundation soil and perlite with pebbles used judiciously here and there.

Koellikeria erinoides, the central plant, grows spikes loaded with little flowers which have a nearly red hood and a broad white frilled lip. It is not an everbloomer, but when one part of the plant gives out another part starts up, so that, with a little manipulation, you can have nearly continuous bloom, especially in winter. And it is so airy and pretty that you will want to have it. The soil should be moist but never wet. It likes to roam a bit but grows quite slowly, forming underground rhizomes, from which new plants arise, as it goes. It is very shallow rooted.

The others are all related miniatures gesneriads—'Little Imp,' 'Pink Petite' (the middle-size flower), 'Doll Baby' (the large ones), and 'White Sprite' (the tiniest).

Dracaenas are among the easiest of foliage plants, so it is a pleasure to report that some are suitable for terrariums. Most can be bought very young but not all are exceptionally attractive. A new hybrid, *Cordyline (Dracaena) terminalis* 'Baby Doll', is a real beauty. It is distinguished by the neon rosy band along the edges of the leaves. The color glows best when the plant receives good light.

We have never favored crowding big bottles or open vessels with a mass of foliage plants. True, the first impression may be pleasant enough, and if one has never seen anything better it may send one into ecstasies. But these "collections" are in their way as pernicious as the cactus dish gardens. The plants are too crowded for their own good and within a short while they grow sufficiently to become unsightly. The terrarium then assumes the aspect of an impenetrable mass of leaves of all kinds pressing against the glass as if they were trying to escape.

Here our big Pyrex column holds nothing but 'Baby Doll,' Begonia 'Cleopatra,' and the fuzzy greenery of a miniature Artillery Plant, *Pilea depressa*. As you see, one tall plant is sufficient. And the other plants are there principally to cover the lower parts of the Dracaena, which loses its leaves with time.

This glass Pyrex column is 24 inches high and 12 inches in diameter. It is a magnificent subject for a well-lighted corner on the floor. The unusual height permits the use of tall material and angled plantings.

A finely grown *B.* 'Sachsen,' which usually bears a few of its small blooms, trails gracefully from the top of the pile. And, down below, we have set two small plants, one of *Serissa foetida variegata,* and an Asparagus Fern *Asparagus plumosus.* The last is a pretty active vine but can be kept under control by frequent trimming. It has the featheriest of all foliage—finer than any fern.

By setting a large rock quite low over the foundation soil and building up the composition very steeply, a dramatic effect is achieved with minimal plant material. This terrarium need not be covered and can be watered regularly if you choose.

Sinningia 'Freckles' looks out from a small plastic cube.

This two-part plastic bubble, 16 inches in diameter, comes from Lucidity. The bottom half rests on a plastic ring and there is a one inch hole in the top half.

In foundation soil we have made a simple planting of Episcias, among which are to be found some of the most beautiful foliage plants. The one on the left is E. 'Cygnet,' whose foliage is the least attractive of this genus. In compensation it has, for the size of a young plant, large, beautifully fringed white flowers. 'Shimmer' the big one in the center is a rather shy bloomer. Most of this type have small, brilliant tomato-red flowers, though there are some with pinks, too. The small one in front, is E. 'Cleopatra,' extraordinary for its light coloring. After a while in the terrarium, 'Cleopatra' will spread a bit and stiffen up, whereupon it is one of the handsomest of all our indoor plants. The varied tones in this terrarium are suggestive of the infinite possibilities with plants of this type.

This is one of the most original of the plastic terrariums and is part of a line which comes with a kit containing soil and seeds of foliage and succulent plants. The base is of bright orange plastic and the inset globe with opening is of clear plastic. The base has a hole for drainage.

As we had no time to germinate the seeds and grow them we decided to show how such a container can be used *after* you have had fun with the seeds. This is a situation which faces many of those who buy kits. Once the original planting has grown or worn out what does one do with them?

In this instance we have found that our *Fittonia verschaffelti* with its red veining fits very well. The plant can be trimmed easily and will grow quite slowly. With a little encouragement it produces a spike of small yellow flowers.

Egg-shaped terrarium and *Fittonia*.

A Tillandsia, a small
bromeliad, on a cactus
skeleton makes a live
sculpture in a clock-
dome terrarium. It is
by Mrs. Rosalia Rau
of New York.

Our picture shows the ingenious way in which Rosalia Rau of New York prepared her bromeliads for enclosure in a dome terrarium.

The upright standard is a cactus skeleton. Friends in the southwest collect these for Mrs. Rau and send them to her for the purpose. Driftwood, cork, tree fern, and other materials with an interesting or natural look can be used. The cactus skeleton is notable for its gray color and the symmetrical hollow openwork of the stem.

Mrs. Rau mixes a quantity of plaster of paris with water and puts it in a plastic sandwich bag. While still soft she fits it into the base of the terrarium. It hardens rather quickly but, while still pliable, the cactus skeleton and an attractive small stone are set into the plaster and held in position for a few minutes until it has hardened.

The bromeliad plant roots are wrapped in a small piece of sheet moss tied with thin wire to the skeleton. Larger pieces of sheet moss are laid over the plaster in the bag to cover the white surface. And, finally, a small piece of driftwood is hung at an angle, from the skeleton, so that it rests on the moss.

On goes the dome and—presto—you have a terrarium.

B.L. Design's dome terrarium holds a florist shop Christmas Kalanchoe, which will bloom for months in this protected environment. Charming as they are, these terrariums have too little space for soil and serve only for the display of a single plant.

Plastic Bubble from Lucidity with cactus and succulent garden.

The plastic bubble has been planted with a few interestingly varied succulents. The general plan is the same as the tank garden. Perlite covers the foundation soil. The whole arrangement is tilted to display the plants and small rocks. Such a terrarium can go a year with no more attention than a light watering every few weeks. *Below*.

This mini-terrarium by B.L. Designs is a charming housing for a single small plant of *Sinningia* 'Bright Eyes.' The plastic cube locks lightly into the opaque plastic base. If at any time your plant outgrows the cube the positions can be reversed. Then the clear cube becomes a pedestal into which the bottom of the pot is supported.

The pot has been filled with sphagnum moss which is just moist. As the only opening in the cube is a slot in the base the moisture is well retained for long periods. This plant has been growing in the terrarium for two months without any attention at all, and some weeks after the photograph was taken we counted eight blooms, each of which lasts for at least two weeks. We expect that it will stay perfectly happily in this housing for the better part of a year—perhaps more. The plant has been under fluorescent light at a distance of about 15 inches. A more carefree method of growing can hardly be imagined.

A "rock," which is really a very large piece of limestone slag from the old ironworks in northwestern Connecticut, had lain piled in the woods for years. Brought home, placed on a bed of perlite in a rubber saucer and covered with a plastic dome, it soon developed moss and ferns from spores which were in it. The advantage of such slags is that they are very light in weight and porous. Thus they can be hollowed out with ease and planted with more exotic material than we have chosen to do here. However, these ferns and mosses have flourished for several years. The small massed fern on the left has been identified as a form of Nephrolepis, or Boston Fern. How it got on the rock is a mystery. It has never grown higher than three or four inches. The slag plays the same role in this terrarium as a foundation mix. That's its plastic dome on the left side.

The double terrarium in its holder of mirror finished metal makes a charming decoration for dinner table, sideboard, or shelving under fluorescent light. Two foliage plants, a Maranta and a variegated fern in small pots, have been set in the plastic flowerpots below and the glass balls inverted over them. The duck is a filler. Looks like a wonderful old oiled-wood decoy duck and is really an extremely skillful Italian imitation in ceramic.

Sinningia 'Poupee' in one globe of B.L. Designs "Executive Model."

The stand has a mirror chrome finish and openings for two plastic pots into which fit two glass globes of the type used for lighting fixtures. With miniature greenery or flowering plants this unit will look well on desk, dining table, or sideboard. As a matter of fact its designer and manufacturer B.L. Designs calls it the Executive Model.

We have planted the one on the left with *Sinningia* 'Poupee' and the one on the right with *xGloxinera* 'Pink Petite.' With time they will grow bigger and produce more flowers at one time.

The terrarium is 30 inches long and 13½ inches wide. Four standards support the lighting fixture which is adjustable as to height. It is designed and built by Environmental Arts of Coconut Grove, Florida, and is the best model we have seen. The planting is awfully busy. But here you have the two essentials for ideal terrarium gardening—a handsome glass case and adequate artificial lighting.

Another terrarium by Environmental Arts, this time with the fluorescent fixtures and tubes built into the cover.

Another terrarium with commercial fluorescent fixture with reflector. A little plastic cube holds a single plant.

Terrariums with Live Sphagnum Moss

We have described sphagnum moss on page 16 along with other houseplant media. As we said, it comes in three forms, alive, the dried plant, and milled. The milled form is sometimes used as a substitute for peat moss in houseplant mixes and is an excellent propagating medium. The other two can constitute the foundation "soil" of specialized terrariums. The action of the dried and live materials is similar, but we prefer the live plants because of our experience that the dried ones compact excessively and soon become a rather unpleasant mush. With proper care live sphagnum will continue to grow.

We show two views of this snifter whose only "soil" is live sphagnum moss. It is a good demonstration of how profusely our plants bloom under these conditions. Because of the small size of the container we have not used any drainage material. The moss has been packed in so that it fills all the spaces but without being tamped down. Just enough water was added to moisten the moss completely. Then the whole was covered with a neatly cut piece of clear plastic. It can be left that way for months at a time.

The principal plant is *Begonia prismatocarpa,* and for once we had a plant in top bloom for the occasion of our photo. You can see how thoroughly the flowers smother the plant. In addition we have a plant of *Sinningia* 'Freckles' and a few *Sinningia pusillas.* All will bloom constantly without any fertilizer. All are planted directly in the sphagnum moss.

Here no attempt is made to have a scene. Nor do we mind the crowding. Every plant being a bloomer, our object is a completely filled flowering picture. Sphagnum moss does not lend itself to sculptural effects. An excess of foliage would look ridiculous but the flowers in such profusion are great.

For terrariums with carnivorous plants (see our plant lists), sphagnum is the only reliable medium. Some of our other house-plants do extremely well in it—especially those which are epiphytic (growing on trees in nature).

Sphagnum has a number of disadvantages. First of all is its limited uses. Secondly, the difficulty for many people of securing the live plants. And thirdly, being essentially a plant cushion, it is difficult to manipulate and control. If you use the dead plant, it will sink and consolidate. If you use the live one, it will often grow as rapidly as your other plants, or more so. Rocks sink into it. And so you are obliged to pack it into a terrarium on the level or, at best, angle it from a low frontal position upward toward the back. The photograph below shows such a planting. This is a terrarium very difficult to keep in a neat condition. The minuscule leaves of the sphagnum are always breaking off and attaching themselves to leaves of plants and to the pane of glass. In spite of all these problems, sphagnum moss terrariums can be things of beauty.

The planting of a sphagnum terrarium is very simple. First you lay down one inch of limestone or marble chips for drainage (it should be limey if possible but charcoal chips will do). Then you

pack in your moss to any depth you desire. Always leave room for plants to grow upward. Compress only lightly. The moss should stay spongy.

Carnivorous plants, which usually come with a ball of sphagnum attached to their roots, are simply poked into the sphagnum. Remove most of the soil from the roots of other plants and just press them into the moss. They will root themselves rapidly.

Sphagnum moss does not tolerate chlorine or other chemicals. Therefore allow your tap water to stand for a few minutes before using. To start with, the right amount of water for the terrarium using live sphagnum should be a thin visible film always present in the drainage. It should not cover the drainage and it should never disappear entirely for long. The sphagnum needs it and it acts like a wick carrying up just enough moisture to your flowering and foliage plants. Dried sphagnum is thoroughly soaked for an hour before using, then wrung out by hand and packed in just like the live material. The amount of water to be added is also the same.

Plants in a sphagnum terrarium require a minimum of fertilizer. Carnivorous plants should not be fertilized at all. If you put a slice of apple or other ripe fruit in the terrarium along with them, fruit flies will be drawn to the plants and provide them with their nourishment. For your regular tropical plants you can supply a very small amount, and very mild solution, of high phosphate and potash fertilizer every three months.

Sphagnum collected in a bog and planted in a terrarium will be a tangle to start with. But within a few weeks new rosettes of leaves appear and, under ideal conditions, the whole surface of the moss will become a light green fluff. If the plants start to grow too high, just poke them down with a stick.

All the plant material you will use in this kind of terrarium prefers a temperature between 65° and 75° Fahrenheit, and you will have to keep it above the lowest limit and open up the terrarium if the temperature goes much higher than 80°. But, for most of the year, a sphagnum terrarium remains sealed, even though it develops a tremendous amount of humidity inside, and the glass is constantly steaming or even dripping. A quality of sphagnum, which has not been analyzed, counteracts fungal growths harmful to plants, and we can therefore ignore the warnings on this point given on the subject of foliage and flowering terrariums.

Terrariums without Foundation Soil for Display and Growing

In giving a step-by-step account of how we put together two larger terrarium plantings, our purpose was to provide basic information useful to the reader no matter what kind of container or arrangement he may have in mind. Not only is our concept of an attractive landscaping quite different from something *you* may want to do; it is also only one of innumerable possible systems. We will be happy if, having read this book, you can go your own way with terrariums.

Terrariums with foundations and landscapes, or at least arrangements of plants in pots in soil, do not exhaust the possibilities. The terrarium principle works extremely well when *only* pots, plants, and stagings are used. By this we mean plants in pots arranged for growing or display in a terrarium-type container. As long as that container is kept partly closed, the plants will benefit in the same way as if they were surrounded by foundation soil, and will need just as little attention. The merit of the principle is demonstrated by the fact that indoor gardeners revive sick plants by putting them, pot and all, into plastic bags or storage boxes for a while.

The terrarium with *just* plants in pots can be attractive because of the framing, the pots being ornamental and the plants carefully groomed. It is clear that where other features do not distract, the plants must be kept in more perfect condition in order to achieve a happy effect than is the case in a landscape terrarium. In these terrariums you can use different kinds of pavings, artistic supports, or stands for the plants, small art objects, and beautiful natural objects, such as shells, figurines, mineral specimens, and so forth. Here, as with the landscapes, and with less trouble, you can make a lovely picture.

We often make this kind of terrarium when we have a plant with an unusually beautiful shape or one that has been trained something like bonsai. In a landscape it is often difficult to do justice to its outstanding quality which is brought out much better if it is displayed alone. This is especially true of a flowering plant. Normally flowers are larger, more numerous, and longer lasting in a terrarium.

Herbs grow particularly well in a terrarium and become ornamental objects in the process. A number of manufacturers now produce kits and containers in various sizes and shapes just for herbs. The photograph shows a two part glass container. The lower section is shaped like an apothecary jar and is fitted with a large round globe.

The plant illustrated is a basil whose seeds were imported from France. It is small-leaved, bushy, fast growing, easily propagated, and delicate of flavor. Most of the basils in the domestic seed catalogs soon grow rather

large for a container of this size. A small-leaved flexible plant adapts itself to the confined space far better than a large-leaved type with stiff stems. As this basil produces quantities of branches it can be trimmed back regularly and the fresh leaves used in the kitchen. A great place for a small or large herb terrarium is on your kitchen work space beneath a cupboard to which a fluorescent fixture has been attached. The plants will grow vigorously in quite small pots. *Container by B.L. Designs.*

This is the herb tank thriving under a fluorescent fixture in our kitchen. The terrarium not only offers the best growing conditions but protects the plants against marauding cats, accidental joggling during kitchen work, and kitchen fumes. They lend an air of elegance and haute cuisine to the simplest kitchen setup.

Just as an arrangement, herbs are a visual delight. In the same foundation-less terrarium used for more formal display we show a collection of herbs. These are, left to right, rosemary, marjoram, basil, winter savory, and thyme. All have been grown entirely under fluorescent light. As you can see, herbs don't have to look messy in the house. They can be both the cook's delight and a showpiece anywhere in the house.

We are using our 5-gallon all-glass tank to demonstrate terrariums without foundation soil. Perlite is spread thinly on the bottom and Japanese pebbles laid over it.

This kind of terrarium is not just for display, although it serves very well for this purpose. The humid and regulated conditions which are so desirable prevail here too. We find that tropical plants, especially the blooming ones, perform better here and more regularly. This is especially true in the city.

Thus the terrarium becomes a place where delicate plants receive special consideration. At the same time it is, of course, very easy to change an arrangement. And, for this reason, a single one of these tanks can do duty continuously, as if it were a vase you keep filled with various flower arrangements.

Here we see *Biophytum sensitivum,* that remarkable little member of the Oxalis family, displaying its symmetry so much like a small palm. On the right is *Gesneria cuneifolia,* the red-flowered everbloomer. And in front is another Oxalis, *O. martiana aureo-reticulata.* This last is one of the most beautiful of all foliage plants and has dark pink blooms in the bargain. However, as soon as light is withdrawn it folds its leaves. And here it is doing just that. The snail is not a menace. And the rock is ruby in tanzanite.

In our all-glass tank 'Doll Baby' is just starting to bloom and *Portulacaria afra-variegata* which, like all higher plants *does* bloom, will remain like a lovely miniature jade tree. The "stone" is a piece of slag, glassy in texture, from an old iron furnace in Connecticut.

For this series of terrariums without foundation soil we are using our 5-gallon all-glass tropical fish tank. The white border of the panes is of plastic and serves to protect the edges. It is removable but we have left it there for the present.

We have used a single trailing Begonia plant, some white Japanese pebbles for the pavement, and three stones. That is all. You can make such an arrangement in a few minutes' time and the Begonia will thrive far better within than outside the tank in a normal apartment environment. Also, since the plant requires very little light to produce its pretty foliage, it can be illuminated by a reading lamp on a side table. Just leave the lamp on for most of the day.

Orchids often require very special conditions. Many of them, for instance, go through cycles when they need a fair amount of watering followed by a period of dryness. Mixing them in with moisture-loving plants such as gesneriads can be rather difficult. But this terrarium has been set up to show how we do accomplish this trick without endangering any of the plants. The terrarium, therefore, was planned to have an orchid, malpighias, which can stand quite a bit of moisture, and an aloe which can do very well without it.

On this occasion we had a plant of *Oncidium ornithorhynchium* in bloom, with two pseudobulbs and four sprays of pink "Dancing Girls," as they are called. The flowers are long lasting and possess an odor which some consider a perfume and others find too powerful. After blooming, a period of dryness is advisable. At no time should this plant have wet feet, but it does enjoy high humidity.

Malpighia coccigera, the Barbados Holly, looks just like a little holly shrub and bears flowers so much like some Oncidium Orchids that botanists are concerned with the question of which is imitating which. So the combination of plants is something of a conversation piece. *Malpighia* is a much prized bonsai plant. Within a few weeks of this planting they were both loaded with delicate pink flowers.

The Aloe is typical of most juvenile aloes—thick leaved, spotted, and slow growing.

By eliminating soil entirely we have avoided the problem of excess moisture and provided a situation where we can water each plant separately with no danger of its seeping from one to the other.

This solution is much the same as that of the set arrangements of two or three pots with the pots showing. The difference is that we have created a stony landscape, the pots are hidden by rocks, and the plants appear to be growing among them. This type of terrarium, if it is not to be too heavy to handle, is planned to be seen from one side only. In the back the pots can be seen. But it has the advantage that they can be removed and handled without any disturbance whatsoever to the arrangement.

The layer of perlite on the bottom is quite thin and the rocks are placed around in an interesting way before the plants are set in place. Then other rocks are added, usually smaller ones, to complete the design and fill in spaces where the pots might be seen. The result is a study in contrasting textures which is most attractive and which will stay that way for a long time.

7 ✿

Lists of
Flowering Plants

Foliage Plants for the Terrarium

No list of foliage plants for the terrarium is likely to be exhaustive, as there are new introductions almost every season. We believe that we have included most of the important and, above all, available plants. We list mostly botanical names as the only reliable ones, though we mention occasionally a well-established common name. Of some of these genera the number of cultivars (hybrids and selections) are legion. These, at least, are usually registered commercial names. Some nurserymen, however, habitually invent names for some of the common plants when a known common name is not available. By giving them a pretty-sounding title they hope to make them more appealing to the buyer and, often, to suggest a beauty and usefulness the plants really do not possess. If you run into this sort of thing, always insist on the shop or nursery labeling your plant with the correct botanical epithet. This is the only reliable way of knowing whether you have the plant you wanted to buy and of propagating it and passing it on to others by its proper name.

Most of the listings are by alphabet. Some large groups, like the

112

bromeliads, orchids, succulents, palms, and ferns, are grouped under general headings.

Acorus gramineus variegatus.   Variegated green and white grasslike foliage. Tufted habit and slow growing. Like a miniature Spider Plant.

Aglaonema.   A genus of Asiatic foliage plants with many species. Growth is single-stemmed, the leaves being plain or spotted and blotched with silver or yellow. When small they are suitable for terrarium use and grow slowly. Some of the species are *A. commutatum albo-variegatum, costatum, hospitum, modestum, pictum, pseudobracteatum, treubi.*

Alternanthera.   "Jacob's Coat." Dwarf plants with colorful, usually twisted, little leaves in pinks and reds. Species commonly available are *A. bettzickiana* and *A. bettzickiana aurea nana, versicolor,* and *amoena.* Six inches maximum.

Aucuba japonica.   The "Gold Dust Plant" and others. Leaves splashed with yellow. The standard type is *A. japonica variegata.* There are a number of variations with different markings. Only the juvenile plants are suitable for a terrarium.

Begonia.   I am indebted to Mr. Jack Golding for the following list of small begonias suitable for terrariums. In addition there are innumerable hybrids.

B. acaulis	*B. mazae viridis*
B. acida	*B. metachroa*
B. acutifolia	*B. nummulariifolia*
B. aridicaulis	*B. olsoniae*
B. boisiana	*B. plebeja*
B. bowerae	*B. prismatocarpa*
B. bowerae nigramarga	*B. rex hybrids*
B. chimborazo	*B. richardsiana*
B. conchifolia, var. *zip*	*B. robusta*
B. cubensis	*B. rotundifolia*
B. decandra	*B. scandens*
B. domingensis	*B. schmidtiana*
B. dregei	*B. solananthera*
B. fagifolia	*B. subnummularifolia*
B. ficicola	*B. sutherlandii*
B. foliosa	*B. teuscheri*
B. herbacea	*B. versicolor*
B. kenworthyae	*B. violifolia*
B. mazae	

The begonias make beautiful subjects for the terrarium and their culture is simple. Many of the above plants bear flowers, especially the famous *B. prismatocarpa,* which is tiny and whose chrome yellow blooms cover the plant. Nevertheless they are principally used for their foliage which is infinitely varied.

Bertolonia.   Medium-size plants with attractive foliage purplish in color. Species are *B. pubescens, maculata, mosaica,* and *marmorata.*

Biophytum sensitivum.   A member of the Oxalis family which looks like a miniature palm or sensitive plant. Symmetrical, pretty and unusual.

Bromeliads.   This huge family of American epiphyte-succulents offers many curious miniatures. *Cryptanthus* are a sort of earth star with brown banded leaves and succulent habit which are most attractive. They require a fairly dry terrarium. Species are *C. zonatus, zebrinus, sebrinus roseus pictus, fosteriana,* and many others. Another interesting genus is *Tillandsia* which runs to spiky and twisted paper shapes. There are very numerous species including *T. bulbosa, caput-medusae,* and *ionantha. Ionantha* is a little spiky plant which turns brilliant red when about to flower. The flowers themselves are insignificant. Most of these grow best attached to wood, cork, or tree fern and may be enclosed as separate specimens as in our illustration on p. 95.

Buxus.   Box. *B. microphylla japonica* and *B. harlandii* are tiny boxwood shrubs, famous for slow growth. Small dark green leaves on a twiggy shrublet.

Cacti.   So numerous are the species that it is impossible to recommend any one in particular. From any cactus specialist nursery you can buy many compact types and will follow your own taste in choosing them. They will not bloom in your terrarium which must, of course, be of the cactus-succulent type.

Calathea.   Calatheas are Marantas with exquisitely stenciled leaves. There are both small- and large-leaved species. These are much more spectacular than the standard "Prayer Plant." Look for interesting species. Among the best are *C. insignis, micans, picturata, trifasciata,* and *van den heckei.* These are all fairly small —up to 8 inches.

Callisia elegans ornata.   Watery-leaved and stemmed plants which trail and grow rather too rapidly. The narrow leaves are striped in light green and silver.

Chamaeranthemum.   Low, spreading, oval-leaved plants prettily marked. Good species are *C. alatum, igneum, godichaudii,* and *venosum.* Four inches.

Codiaeum punctatum and *punctatum aureum.*   The "Apple-leaved Croton." Rather stiff, with narrow wavery leaves marked with yellow. Single-stemmed.

Coleus blumei and hybrids.   Coleus often looks garish in a terrarium but when quite small it may fit in nicely.

Coprosma baueri.   Simple-leaved shrubs which when very small can be planted in a terrarium.

Cordyline terminalis.   Ti plants or Dracaenas. Very young plants
   of 'Florida Beauty' or 'Baby Doll' are stiff but attractive in a
   tall terrarium.
Ctenanthe.   Closely related to *Calathea. C. oppenheimiana tricolor*
   is a beauty, as is *C. glabra.* The hybrid called 'Burle Marx,' after
   the great Brazilian garden architect, is very choice and compact.
Cymbalaria muralis. Kenilworth Ivy.   This little creeper is useful
   as a ground cover.
Dichorisandra.   Pretty purple and silver leaves and fleshy stems.
   Trails and is a fast grower.
Diosma reevesii.   A heatherlike shrublet.
Dracaena.   Single-stemmed plants which are only useful when very
   young. Species with attractive spreading leaves are *D. godsef-
   fiana, goldieana* and *sanderiana.*
Eleagnus pungens.   A shrub with oval leaves. *E. pungens variegata*
   is margined with white. Only very small plants are useful.
Euonymus.   When small these common outdoor shrubs with very
   small leaves will fit in a terrarium. Suitable species are *E. japon-
   icus albo-marginatus, media picta, microphyllus. E.* 'Silver
   Queen' is one of many hybrids and selections.
Ferns.   The following are the most commonly used in terrariums.
   As they all grow large roots they should be confined in pots.
      Adiantum bellum, capillus-veneris, caudatum, cuneatum,
   and *macrophyllum.*
      Asparagus plumosus.   The Asparagus Fern is not a fern
   but is usually included in the lists because of its delicate foliage.
      Asplenium nidus-avis.   The Bird's-nest Fern. Only little
   ones of course.
      Davallia bullata and *pentaphylla.*
      Nephrolepis exaltata.   Boston Fern. Finely cut varieties,
   among others, are *N.* 'Whitmanii' and 'Norwoodii.'
      Polystichum tsus-sinense.   A favorite for miniature gar-
   dens.
      Pteris cretica albo-lineata and *ensiformis* 'Victoriae.'
   There are many "Table Ferns" which can be used in terrariums.
Ficus pumila (or *repens*) is a miniature fig vine with flat little leaves
   which will attach themselves to the glass of your terrarium.
   Must be kept under control. *F. diversifolia* is a little shrub
   bearing round green fruits.
Fittonia.   Spreading low plants with attractively veined leaves.
      F. argyroneura has leaves intricately veined in white, while *F.*
      verschaffeltii is red-veined. Four inches.
Geogenanthus undatus.   A trailer with heart-shaped leaves striped
   with gray.
Gynura aurantiaca.   This is not truly a terrarium plant but young
   cuttings look very attractive in plantings with their fuzzy purple leaves. Keep trimmed.

Hedera helix.   Ivy. There are innumerable small-leaved plain and variegated ivies. Very slow growing they are among the best vines for the terrarium. Nurseries usually have many kinds to choose from.

Helxine soleiroli.   Baby's Tears. A good ground cover.

Hemigraphis colorata.   Metallic purple leaves. Height maximum six inches.

Homalomena wallisii.   Rather broad flat mottled leaves. Six inches.

Hoya.   Hoyas are succulents and mostly vines, which grow very slowly along with other foliage plants in a terrarium. The Wax Plant, *H. carnosa variegata,* is green and white with red stems and red young growth. *H. minima* is much smaller and has almost round fleshy green leaves.

Hypoestes sanguinolenta.   The Freckle-faced Plant. Heart-shaped leaves are polka-dotted in pink. One of the easiest plants to grow and rather too rapid. Keep it trimmed.

Iresine.   Bloodleaf. Little plants variegated with red or purple. Rather messy looking but colorful. Four inches.

Malpighia coccigera.   This miniature "holly" from the Caribbean is unlikely to bear its beautiful little pink flowers but its bright shiny green foliage and branching shrubby habit are very attractive.

Maranta leuconeura kerchoveana is the Prayer Plant with chocolate-blotched oval leaves. *M. leuconeura massangeana* is much more spectacular in its design—like a peacock feather. *M. bicolor* and *repens* are two other useful species.

Myrsine africana.   Like box but less stiff. Small leaved. Also *M. nummularia.* Slow growing but keep trimmed.

Osmanthus ilicifolius variegatus.   Chinese Holly. Variegated with white. Shrubby.

Palms.   *Chamaedorea elegans* and *tenila* can be purchased as 4- or 5-inch plants and will last a while in a terrarium.

Pellionia daveauana and *pulchra.*   Trailing plants with leaves lying flat along the branches and interestingly variegated in brownish shades.

Peperomia.   Although some are pretty stiff little plants Peperomias sometimes come in useful for the terrarium. In most species the growth of the leaves and their stems appears to be directly out of the soil so that they remain pretty much at the same height —4 to 8 inches. There are a wealth of varieties sufficiently dwarf for our purposes. To mention a few—*P. petiolata, caprata, obtusifolia,* and *verschaffeltii. P.* 'Astrid' is a pretty miniature.

Philodendron.   Popular as they are, Philodendrons are not too good for a terrarium. *P. micans* and *andreanum* might be considered.

Pilea.   Pileas such as *P. cadierei,* the Aluminum Plant, have upright growth. Others of the Artillery Plant type are more prostrate and serve as good fillers and ground covers. Among these are *P. depressa, involucrata, microphylla.* The hybrid 'Silver Tree' is bushy.

Plectranthus australis Swedish Ivy. Rather coarse hanging plant with white flowers. Other *Plectranthus* have, like *P. coleoides* and *marginatus,* variegated foliage. *P. oertendahlii* with a bronzy leaf, is a good-looking plant. But they are all rather rank growers for the terrarium.

Polyscias (Aralia). The Parsley Aralias grow into impressive "institutional" plants but young cuttings, because of the fine-cut foliage and slow growth, are very useful. Best for the purpose is *P. fruticosa elegans.* Other species are *P. balfouriana, filicifolia,* and *guilfoylei.*

Pothos. This is a name applied usually to *Scindapsus aureus* 'Marble Queen,' a popular, thick-leaved, variegated, white and green, small vine. All right for the terrarium in a pinch.

Rosmarinus prostratus and *officinalis.* Rosemary does fine in a terrarium as long as it is kept moist. In our experience *R. officinalis,* the upright type, is superior. It is easy to trim and keep neat.

Sansevieria 'Hahnii.' This dwarf Snake Plant is all right for a rather stiff arrangement. It will certainly grow slowly. There is a 'Green Hahnii' and a 'Silver Hahnii.'

Saxifraga sarmentosa. Strawberry Geranium. Neither a strawberry nor a geranium, this is a very pretty plant with a rosette of round leaves. Var. *tricolor* is banded with white and pink. A fine plant for the terrarium if you watch out for those long stolons it sends out and with which it gets new plants started all over the place. Cut them back as soon as they appear.

Scilla violacea. The only bulb plant of the Lily family we can mention for terrariums. The narrow leaves are fleshy and exquisitely mottled in light and dark green. It grows neatly and spreads.

Selaginella. The Selaginellas are feathery-foliaged, flat-growing plants which do well in the shade and in high humidity. *S. uncinata* is remarkable for the touches of a strange blue in among the green. *S. kraussiana* and *plumosa* are other good types. The Selaginellas make magnificent ground covers but are not easy to maintain. One problem is that they require rather cool temperatures. If you can master them you will be delighted with their beauty.

Serissa foetida variegata. A small shrub with small leaves bordered with white. Easy and manageable.

Streptocarpus holstii. This fleshy-stemmed gesneriad has classic jade green leaves. Keep it trimmed and it will be an adornment.

Succulents. The succulent plants are so numerous and varied that our only advice is to pick them out at nurseries by their appear-

ance. Most of them will stay healthy in a cactus-succulent terrarium if provided with plenty of light. Rosette types should
generally be avoided because of their tendency to lose their
shape and become elongated unless the light is of greater in-
tensity than you can provide.

Flowering Plants for the Terrarium

Because the possibility of flowering plants in terrariums is relatively
new, very few of those we use for the purpose are sold in flower
shops, and it may be a number of years still before they will be
available there. In the meanwhile, a number of nurseries, scattered
across the country, propagate and sell them. The names of these
firms will be found in the list of sources.

Our listing of flowering plants will begin with the gesneriad
family (*Gesneriaceae*), of which the African Violet is the most popular member and which, more than any other, has contributed to
the new wave. Other plants and plant families follow in alphabetical
order. Mention is also made of a few categories which it is not
advisable to try to bloom, simply because many readers will ask
whether they can. Miniature Roses and Geraniums are examples of
this.

As many of the plants are unfamiliar to most readers we will
describe them in some detail except where this has already been
done elsewhere in the book. Light requirements are stated in distance from a 24-inch, 20-watt, two-tube fluorescent fixture lighted
for about sixteen hours a day.

The Gesneriads

Codonanthe. Of this genus the most interesting species has been
    introduced within the last year and bears the tentative name
    of C. *ventricosa.* Rather thin stiff trailing stems, some 6 inches
    long, fan out from the pot, with roundish hairy opposite little
    leaves spaced along their lengths. The flowers are only ½-inch
    long, white, and the shape of a widemouthed cone. They
    are pleasantly fragrant and last up to a week on the stem.
    A species with more lax stems, shiny, very dark green leaves,
    and 1-inch-long trumpets still lacks a name. C. *macradenia* and
    crassifolia, which have been in culture for a longer period,
    have oval shiny leaves of larger size and longer stems. The
    rather large white tubular flowers last only a day. *Codonanthe*
    likes a humid atmosphere but soil which is moist, not wet. It
    can bloom up to 18 inches from the fixture.
Columnea. As a trailing basket plant with its flaming 3-to-4-
    inch long-lasting Goldfish flowers, *Columnea* is the most gor-

geous of greenhouse and houseplants. As such they won't do
for terrariums. In the last couple of years more upright hybrids
have been introduced and are fine additions to our repertoire.
Some are everblooming. And a most useful feature is that cuttings of blooming branches root themselves rapidly and continue to bloom under terrarium conditions. They will do so
15 to 20 inches under lights.

Columnea performs best in moist, but not wet, very light
porous soil. Best of the medium-size hybrids is C. 'Chanticleer.'
'Early Bird,' 'Mary Ann,' 'Twiggy,' 'Yellow Dragon,' and 'Yellow Gold' are relatively easy. Columneas must be trimmed back
rigorously. They always hang a bit once the stems reach a length
of 6 inches—even the stiffest of them. Let them trail from a high
point in the terrarium.

Episcia. The Episcias are notable for the beauty of their leaves
and for that alone are worthwhile using in a terrarium. Due to
their trailing habit and rather rapid growth they don't last too
long. So start out with juvenile rooted cuttings and you will
have at least the good part of a year to admire them. The flowers, orange, pink, or white, though small, light up the plant.

Of the two plants we recommend as best, one is not typical
and the other is still to be marketed. *E.* 'Cygnet' has green scalloped leaves less attractive than other Episcias but a young cutting, 2 inches high, more easily than any other bears white
flowers, beautifully speckled and fringed. If you religiously
remove all suckers that appear, the plant will remain compact
a long time. The second plant is a selection of our own with
brown leaves and tomato-red flowers. It is more compact than
others and holds its blooms well above the foliage.

Of the hybrids in trade 'Moss Agate,' with magnificent quilted
green leaves, and an old favorite, 'Acajou,' are the best. 'Silver
Sheen' is another good one. *E. lilacina* has a thick pile and is
beautifully zoned but you will have difficulty blooming the very
large blue flowers. *E.* 'Cleopatra' is particularly decorative.

Episcias like rich moist soil and rot if soaked too often. Light
requirements vary considerably according to the plant. A foot
from the lights is relatively safe.

Gesneria. A few of these are near perfection as flowering terrarium plants, being compact, slow growing, and incredibly
floriferous. They must be kept constantly wet as one day of dryness is enough to cause collapse. They can be bloomed up to
18 inches from the lights but prefer a position within 15 inches.

G. cuneifolia has shiny spoon-shaped leaves and 1-inch red
tube flowers with a short spreading tip. Maximum height is
about 4 inches. It has two variations. 'Quebradillas' is darker
leaved and the flowers are yellow streaked with red. 'El Yunque'

is yellow-flowered, tipped with orange red. This is our preferred type as the flowers are borne on long pedicels well above the foliage.

G. pedicellaris x citrina. This is a very recent cross made by Michael Kartuz between two very attractive but somewhat more difficult plants. The first has crinkly leaves and pouch-type blood-red upright flowers. *G. citrina* is a shrublet with hanging bell flowers in chrome yellow. Both are well worth growing. The hybrid has the leaves of *cuneifolia* and the same flower habit except that the blossoms are chrome yellow. This remarkable plant is as vigorous, easy, and floriferous as *G. cuneifolia.* It is one of the greatest achievements of modern hybridizing. *G. christii* closely resembles *G. pedicellaris.*

xGloxinera. These are hybrids between miniature Sinningias and Rechsteinerias. They form flat rosettes of leaves and send up 2-inch stems bearing pink trumpets. They are not ever-blooming like some of the Sinningias and do go dormant. However they are small and can be switched in the terrarium once or twice a year. Some of the best are 'Krishna,' 'Little Imp,' 'Pink Flare,' 'Pink Imp,' and 'Pink Petite.' All of these and the others are charming. They bloom 15 or more inches from the lights, like terrarium humidity, and should not be kept too wet. A plant called *xGloxinera* 'Tinkerbell' with narrow red purple tubes is a nice trailer and produces flowers more easily than the others.

Hypocyrta. Until last year Hypocyrtas could not be recommended for terrariums. But that has changed due to the hybridizations of William Saylor.

The old plants were very lax trailers and rather shy bloomers. The new ones are erect growing and bloom more freely. Hypocyrtas have unusual and charming pouch flowers (one of the original species was known as the Candy Corn plant) with a tiny opening up front. The hybrids require just moist conditions and bright light. They will grow a foot high given the chance but when trimmed back they will branch.

H. 'Rio' has green fleshy leaves and hairy orange pouch flowers.

H. 'Tropicana' and 'Mardi Gras' have yellow pouches striped with dark red. The leaves are dark green above and red beneath. 'Mardi Gras' is the more compact plant.

Koellikeria erinoides is described on p. 91. It is desirable for its airy bloom but does not like to stay in its pot. By means of trimming it can be kept in check. As it propagates from rhizomes these can be lifted from their places in the terrarium and replanted. *Koellikeria* needs a high position close to the lights—not more than 5 inches away in most cases. Though, on second thought, we can remember seeing it bloom in poor, almost north window, light; but then the stems became much longer.

Kohleria. These plants have handsome velvety leaves but most of them grow too large and straggly for the terrarium. At most, small plants can grow there for a while and give foliage color. A partial exception is *K. amabilis.* You may be able to bring this one to bloom and enjoy the large pink trumpets with beautiful veining. The plant gets messy after a time and must be cut back, whereupon it starts new growths from underground rhizomes. Blooms about 15 inches from the lights and prefers a moist soil.

Phinaea multiflora. A 3-inch-high mass of fuzzy gray green leaves topped by upfacing white cups on ramrod-stiff pedicels. It grows well in a terrarium, seeds itself, and produces underground rhizomes. As older plants die down new ones come up and can easily be moved to the right spot in the terrarium. It is not a showy plant but a good space filler and rather cute.

Rechsteineria cardinalis. Velvety leaves and long red tube flowers distinguish this tuberous plant which goes dormant after a while. It is good therefore only for a season. *R. leucotricha* has marvelous brushed-silver leaves and pink tube flowers. A most aristocratic plant with the same bad habit of dormancy.

Saintpaulia. African Violet. African Violets come in an incredible range of forms and colors—only yellow being missing. Because there is a constant outpouring of new hybrids on top of an enormous list of older plants, it is quite impossible to single out the plants for you. Some are prettier than others and some are easier to grow. It is best to select plants at a nursery and consult the grower as to the best plants for terrarium culture. There are a great number of miniature plants which take up little room.

African Violets, by and large, do well in terrariums, needing little attention except occasional thinning of the outer leaves, repotting and removing the remains of flowers. Even moisture is what they like. Some varieties will grow and bloom 2 feet from the lights.

Two plants we liked recently have been a miniature called 'Dogwood' with blue flowers on each lobe of which is a nicely placed white spot; and 'Lisa,' a normal-size plant, from Fischer Greenhouses, that produces its solid pink flowers endlessly and is quite a foolproof plant.

Seemannia latifolia. Another perfect terrarium plant. It grows about 5 inches high, has long light green soft leaves and brilliant orange red pouch flowers on long pedicels. Very floriferous and does not go dormant. New plants can be started

from the underground rhizomes. It likes to be about 8 inches
from the lights in high humidity and just moist soil conditions.

Sinningia.   The prize beauty of this genus is *S. speciosa* the Florist
Gloxinia, which is much too big for a terrarium. Fischer Greenhouses does have a dwarf called 'Tom Thumb,' which will fit
in. However, all Gloxinias go dormant after blooming while
the wonderful new generation of *Sinningia* hybrids do not, are
everblooming, and just about perfect for the terrarium, both
for beauty and compactness.

Before listing the hybrids, however, we must mention two
species at the other end of the size scale that are parents in most
of the crosses. These are the tiny Sinningias *pusilla* and *concinna. Pusilla* is about an inch in diameter and sends up 1-inch
stems bearing ½-inch flowers which are bluish trumpets. It
has very little root, blooms continuously, and seeds itself all
over the place. It is indispensable in terrarium plantings. A
sport, 'White Sprite,' which is white of course, is equally useful. *S. concinna* has a little bigger flower, deeper color, and a
throat that is white with purple spots. It is neither as easy nor
as floriferous as *pusilla* and does not reproduce itself automatically. But it is a little beauty.

The hybrids are all a bit larger than the two species and are
colored purple or lavender or bluish. Each is different in detail, and we wish we had more room for descriptions. Each one
is "indispensable." Whenever you are planting a terrarium look
for *S.* 'Bright Eyes,' 'Doll Baby,' 'Freckles,' 'Wood Nymph,'
'Poupee,' and 'Cindy.' 'Cindy' is the loveliest of the bunch,
putting up clusters of handsome trumpets symmetrically striped
and the white throats patterned with purple dots. *S.* 'Snowflake'
is like a 'White Sprite' with a fringe.

All of these require relatively little light and will bloom 10
or more inches away from the lights. They are also not dependent on very high humidity but grow larger blooms in the
terrarium. All are popular and are available from the specialist
nurseres on our list.

Smithiantha.   Scalloped red plush and green leaves make juveniles
useful as foliage color in the terrarium. Only two are small
enough to grow there. The best is *S.* 'Little Tudor' with spires
of curved hanging bell flowers in red and yellow, and the similar
S. 'Little One.' They grow about 5 inches high and must be
kept within 10 inches of the lights. Even moisture is best.

Streptocarpus.   These are long-leaved plants with clusters of trumpets on very long pedicels. The small species are difficult to
grow and the large plants won't fit. However, a wonderful
hybrid, by Frances Batcheller, called 'Constant Nymph,' with
blue flowers, has led to a series of smaller plants of the same
type. These include 'Mini-Nymph' and 'Netta Nymph.' Some

have not yet acquired names. These plants grow about 8 inches across and the stems are 4 to 6 inches high. The flowers are broad trumpets in blue and white with handsome markings. The plants grow very well in sphagnum moss and prefer light soil mixtures to peat mixes. Keep them 12 to 15 inches under the lights.

Other Flowering Plants

Allophyton mexicanum. From low rosettes of spoon-shaped leaves rise little clusters of purplish snapdragonlike flowers. Keep on the wet side. About 15 inches from the lights.

Begonias. Most of these are listed under foliage plants but many will bloom in the terrarium although few of the small plants are very showy. *B. prismatocarpa* is exceptionally floriferous and covers the plant with yellow blooms. *B. weltoniensis* and *B. richardsiana* are attractive and do bloom easily. Stitchleaf and hybrids of the 'Cleopatra' type send up their airy sprays occasionally. However, your best bet is the common Wax Begonia, *B. semperflorens.* Dwarf varieties produce plenty of white, pink, or red flowers but must be trimmed back regularly. Keep them quite moist. Fifteen to 18 inches from the lights is close enough.

Crossandra undulaefolia. Large, very shiny green leaves and fan-shaped ,orange flowers characterize this handsome plant. Grown from cuttings it remains fairly compact and can be trimmed so that it branches and produces more bloom. Keep quite moist and within a foot of the lights.

Cuphea hyssopifolia. This little shrub is quite woody but stays small and produces quantities of pink tiny flowers continuously. Fairly foolproof.

Exacum affine. A member of the Gentian family, with fleshy close-packed leaves and 1/2-inch blue flowers with prominent yellow stamens, produced continuously. A very easy plant which can be up to 18 inches from the lights. Only problem is getting rid of all the dead blossoms. Keep trimmed and neat. An ideal terrarium plant.

Jacobinia carnea. This is a big greenhouse plant which grows compact from cuttings. On a 3-inch-high plant the spike of long pink flowers may be 4 inches high and 3 inches or more in diameter. When the flower stalk is cut off, side branches produce more flowers. Eventually cuttings can be made of budding branches and a new start begun. Does not absorb or like much water. Keep a bit on the dry side. Should be placed about 10 inches from the lights, at most.

Jasminum sambac. 'Maid of Orleans.' A fragrant true Jasmine which perfumes the terrarium and has lovely white pinwheel flowers. Medium moisture and about 12 inches from the lights. Slow growing but trails.

Orchids. Orchids are a chapter in themselves—at least. The possibilities are legion but have thus far been little explored. We know that the Jewel Orchids—Ludisias, Anoectochilus, and so on—with exquisite foliage and spikes of bloom, do well. Lockhartias, which have herringbone leaves and yellow flowers, grow beautifully. From there on you must consult specialty publications as orchids require special culture (though not especially difficult). From the huge lists of species and cultivars choose compact plants that are listed as warm growing. These will usually do well in a terrarium.

Oxalis martiana aureo-reticulata. This Oxalis never goes dormant and has fantastic gold-veined foliage and pink flowers. It will grow and spread too rapidly in a terrarium but young plants will provide six months of charm and contrast. Then break up the plant and start again. Since it consists of a cluster of bulblets, separating a large plant into a number of small ones is just a matter of pulling them apart and potting them up separately. Requires plenty of moisture. Six inches high unless light-starved.

Punica granatum nana. Dwarf Pomegranate. This dwarf tree fits into large terrariums and produces flowers and fruit. Both are something to see—the flowers flaming orange and the fruit apple red. It is graceful and easily trained. Keep within 15 inches of the lights. Everblooming.

Scilla violacea. A member of the Lily family from South Africa, with narrow handsomely mottled leaves and greenish flowers. Succulent in habit it will do well also in a foliage or flowering terrarium.

Plants Not Advisable for Terrariums

Achimenes. At least in the city this wonderful gesneriad does not bloom in or out of the terrarium.

Fuchsias. No success here. Not enough ventilation for one thing and not cool enough at night.

Geraniums. We would dearly like to raise miniature Geraniums in a terrarium and it is possible. All that is required is an internal air conditioner to keep the temperature below 70° most of the year, and lower at night. As this is impossible for most of us—no Geraniums.

Roses. Miniature Roses are ideal plants from the standpoint of size and floriferousness. But, here again, very cool conditions are a must and until we solve that we will have to pass up Roses.

Carnivorous Plants

Everybody would like to raise these fascinating plants and bloom them. Raising them is not too difficult. Blooming is another matter. As discussed in the section on sphagnum terrariums, this moss is the best medium for these plants and almost no attention is required as the terrarium is kept sealed most of the time. Bloom requires that the plants be within a few inches of the lights and temperatures kept moderate. If, on days when the temperature in the room is comfortable and humidity fairly high (50 percent or better), you open the terrarium and leave a piece of fruit on the moss, fruit flies will be attracted and the plants will have a feast. They should not receive other forms of nourishment.

Darlingtonia.   Cobra Plant. *D. californica* is a hooded pitcher plant with a waxed moustache hanging down. They are pretty awful looking but exciting. Since they may reach two feet in size you will probably end up with runts but they will do if they get the whiskers.

Dionaea muscipula.   You can buy Venus's-flytraps in variety stores all packed in sphagnum. It is a small plant and the leaves, tricky as they are, are not large. The flowering stem, however, is a foot long and the bloom is a very simple white-petaled one. Be happy if you keep the toothed leaves coming along.

Drosera.   There are a number of different Sundews, all characterized by small leaves or stems covered with viscid hairs. Being red in color under good light they glisten prettily perched on the sphagnum. Flowers are white or pink.

Pinguicula.   The Butterworts have gelatinous-looking rosettes of leaves which are no attraction except to insects. The flowers, on the other hand, are little horns and very pretty. The largest-flowered is *P. lutea,* which is yellow. There is also a lovely blue one. Not easy to flower.

Sarracenia.   Pitcher Plants or Huntsman's Horns. Straight or curved tubes with a lid or hood. There are a number of kinds. *S. flava* which is sold for terrariums can grow 4 feet high although the huge yellow bloom, growing beside the pitcher, is much lower. If you can get a nice group of medium-size trumpets you will be doing well. *S. psittacina* and *rubra* are smaller plants. *S. purpurea* has a tall handsome flower while the bloom of *rubra* and *psittacina* is shorter and smaller. The pitchers are sufficiently spectacular with their odd colors and veinings. If you can pull off a bloom it will really be a tour de force. Don't count on it.

Hardy Plants for the Terrarium

The plants used for a wild or hardy terrarium are all northern woodland species the removal of which is condemned by conservationists. Although taking a few plants from the woods may seem an insignificant act, when carried on by thousands of other hobbyists and commercial collectors the cumulative effect is noticeable. Normal balance in nature provides that each plant propagate itself so that a one-to-one relationship is continued through the generations. When great numbers of parent plants are destroyed, there is an inevitable and, often, irreplaceable reduction in population. If you wish to plant this type of terrarium buy your live material from professional growers. We do not really know whether they propagate their plants but we hope so.

Club Moss (*Lycopodium*).   There are several northern types available. They are trailing greenery putting up spikes and whorls of narrow or fan-shaped leaves. Not a moss.

Maidenhair Fern (*Adiantum pedatum*).   A beautiful spiral-leaved fern. Unless quite a juvenile it is rather large for a terrarium. Height 12 inches and spread at least 12 inches.

Partridgeberry (*Mitchella repens*).   Tiny-leaved ground trailer that has fuzzy four-petaled flowers and produces quantities of red berries which last all winter long.

Pipsissewa and Princess Pine (*Chimaphila maculata* and *umbellata*). Low plants of the woods, one striped with white and the other dark green. The nodding flowers are white and pink.

Polypody Fern (*Polypodium vulgare*).   Creeping short fern, with 4- to 8-inch leaves.

Rattlesnake Plantain (*Goodyera pubescens*).   An orchid of oak and pine woods which has beautifully white-veined green leaves and spikes of puffy white flowers.

Shinleaf.   Various species of *Pyrola*, usually *P. elliptica*. Rosettes of green leaves that put forth 5-inch spikes of waxy bell flowers.

Trailing Arbutus (*Epigaea repens*).   The famous rough oval-leaved trailer with waxy white to pink flowers and an exquisite fragrance. Requires acid soil.

Walking Fern (*Camptosorus rhyzophyllus*).   A famous, rare, single-leaf fern that forms new plantlets when the tip of its leaf touches the soil. Lime loving.

Unless your culture is perfect none of these plants will actually bloom in your terrarium.

8

Bottle Gardening

Bottle gardening is a delightful side aspect of terrarium gardening. The sight of an elegant foliage collection, a single charming flowering plant, or even a miniature landscape always arouses astonishment. Asked how we get the plants into the bottle we have often answered with straight faces, "But, of course, by cutting away the bottom of the bottle and pasting it on again after we have planted it."

Our good friend F. Vance Fazzino of New York describes in the following pages just how it is done. Mr. Fazzino is a distinguished furniture designer and a master practitioner of the bottle gardening art. His friend Alexander Capodonna has drawn the tools and bottles for us.

BOTTLES

As long as they are of clear glass, bottles of any size may be used, from a small perfume bottle up to a water cooler bottle or carboy. Some other glass containers are those for liquor, wine, cider jugs, pickle jars, and so on. Naturally small bottles will do only for tiny plants—perhaps only a single one. In the larger bottles there can be a whole collection of greenery and some miniature flowering plants.

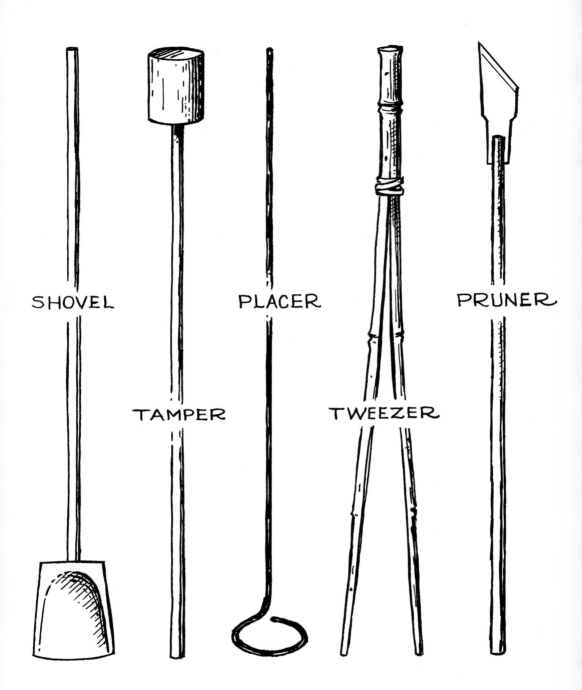

SHOVEL   TAMPER   PLACER   TWEEZER   PRUNER

TOOLS

The tools required for planting and maintaining the bottle garden can be made in a few minutes. But it is understood that those which are suitable for planting large and deep bottles will not work for small ones, and vice versa. If you become an enthusiast, you will have three or four sizes of everything.

1. A funnel made of rolled paper or flexible cardboard and fastened with a staple or tape. The funnel should reach almost to the bottom of the bottle.

2. Straighten out a length of coat hanger and make a loop on one end at right angles. One side of the loop should be open. This is your positioner.

3. A shovel made of a wooden dowel, one end of which is partly hollowed out. A tiny discarded demitasse spoon, its handle stuck into a dowel, is perfect for the larger openings.

4. Long tweezers made of split bamboo. A green garden stake of narrow gauge bamboo is excellent. Split it most of the length and spread at the very top with a strip of rubber inserted in the crack or, in a pinch, a cigarette filter. To prevent the bamboo from splitting all the way to the upper end, it is necessary to tape or tie it tightly at the top of the split.

5. A short piece of broom handle or a cork attached to a dowel acts as a tamper.

SOIL

Use a sterilized garden soil with a good proportion of peat or leaf mold. Commercial packaged soils will do. For drainage, coarse sand or pebbles plus charcoal are best. No fertilizer is necessary.

PLANTS

A list of suggested plants is on the last page. Most of them are foliage plants, modest in size and relatively slow growers. You must gauge your choice of plant to the size of the container. For instance, a little bottle may have room only for a single *Sinningia pusilla*. A carboy will hold a number of the larger plants.

Before placing, be sure that your plants are free of insects. This applies to the soil in which they have been living as well as the plants themselves. It is wise to use a strong magnifying glass for your inspection. Do not use any material that is infested.

PLANTING THE BOTTLE

1. Place the funnel into the bottle so that it almost reaches the bottom.

2. Pour in pebbles, then the charcoal. In a small bottle the depth should be an eighth to a quarter inch. In larger ones, it can be two to three inches. Smaller particles will be needed for the smaller bottle. Shake the bottle so that the drainage is spread evenly.

3. Pour in the soil to a depth of at least a half inch in the small bottles and as much as three or four inches in big ones. Spread and tamp down with your tamper.

4. Decide where the plants are to be placed, allowing for different sizes, rate of growth, and artistic arrangement. For each plant dig a hole with the shovel.

5. Decant the plant from its pot, remove excess soil, and fit the loop of your tool around its neck. Lower it into the bottle and set in place. Remove the loop tool, hold the plant, if necessary, with the tweezers.

6. Clamp the stem of the plant with the tweezers and set it perfectly straight. Remove the excess earth around it. Then tamp all around until the soil is smooth and the plant firmly set.

7. Water through the opening with a sprayer. This will clean the leaves as well as water the soil. Clean the inside of the bottle by spraying along the sides. You may also use a tube and water the sides, thus cleaning away any soil dust. The water level should reach the top of the drainage material at the initial watering. You can see this through the glass.

8. Your bottle garden is now ready and can be covered. Should the surface of the soil continue to be dry the following day, this will be an indication that additional water is needed. If the glass becomes covered with water drops, it means that there is too much. Open the top and leave it that way for a day. Repeat until a light vapor coat appears only at night.

9. Set the bottle on a shelf in the light garden, under a circle light fluorescent tube or on the edge of the light garden, as close to it as possible. The bottle garden will also flourish in an east window, a north window in summer, a south window in summer only if it is curtained. Protect from excessive heat (above 85°) or cold (below 60°).

10. Your bottle garden may not require attention for months at a time. No ventilation is needed. If the plants get out of hand by growing too fast, they can be trimmed with a razor blade tied to the end of a dowel (careful) and the debris picked out with the tweezers. When plants become too big or die, you can remove them with the tweezers and place new plants in the same positions along with a little additional soil.

PLANT LIST

Ferns. Adiantum bellum, A. capillus-veneris, A. cuneatum, Asplenium nidus, Davallia bullata, D. pentaphylla, Nephrolepis (small varieties), *Polystichum tsus-sinense, Pteris cretica,* among others. *Foliage plants. Acorus gramineus variegatus, Alternanthera* (Jacob's Coat), *A. bettzickiana, A. bettzickiana aurea nana, A. versicolor* and *amoena; Calathea micans; Carex variegata; Chaemaeranthemum gaudichaudi, igneum, venosum; Ctenanthe* species; *Dracaena* 'Florida Beauty'; *Ficus pumila minima, F. radicans variegata; Fittonia verschaffelti; Maranta* (small varieties); *Helxine soleiroli* (Baby's Tears);

Homalomena walisii; Pellionia pulchra and *daveauana;* small *Peperomias; Pilea depressa; Selaginella kraussiana* and *uncinata.*

FLOWERING PLANTS

Will bloom if exposed to long hours of fluorescent light. *Allophyton mexicanum;* small foliage Begonias; *Gesneriads,* such as *Boea hygroscopica, Chirita micromusa, Columnea microphylla, Diastema maculate* and *quinquevulnerum,* the *Gesnerias,* x*Gloxineras, Koellikeria erinoides, Kohleria amabilis* and *lindeniana, Phinaea multiflora,* miniature *Saintpaulias,* miniature *Sinningias* and other hybrids, *Streptocarpus cyanandrus, kirki,* and *rimicola;* Miniature Orchid species and hybrids; *Oxalis hedysaroides rubra* (Fire Fern).

SOURCES

Alberts & Merkel, Boynton Beach, Fla. 33435.
Arthur Eames Allgrove, North Wilmington, Mass. 01887.
Kartuz Greenhouses, 92 Chestnut St., Wilmington, Mass. 01887.
Merry Gardens, Camden, Maine 04843.

Sources of Supply

Plant Sources

Abbey Garden, 18007 Topham Street, Reseda, Calif. 91335. Cacti and succulent plants shipped. Catalog.

Alberts & Merkel Bros., Inc., 2210 South Federal Highway, Boynton Beach, Fla. 33435. Orchids, bromeliads, tropical foliage plants and succulents. Catalog 50¢.

Arthur Eames Allgrove, Box 459, Wilmington, Mass. 01887. Woodland terrarium plants and accessories. Terrariums and planters. Catalog.

Arndt's Floral Garden, 20454 N.E. Sandy Boulevard, Troutdale, Oreg. 97060. Gesneriads and other exotic plants. Seeds. List 10¢.

Aunt Dotty's Arbor, 1103 Third Avenue, N.Y., N.Y. 10021. Orchids. No shipping.

Barrington Greenhouses, 860 Clemente Road, Barrington, N.J. 08016. Miniature houseplants.

Beach Garden Nursery, 2131 Portola Drive, Santa Cruz, Calif. 95060. Bromeliads and exotics. No catalog, no shipping.

Bennett's Bromeliads & Bonsai, 1621 Mayfield Avenue, Winter Park, Fla. 32789. List with stamped addressed envelope.

Bolduc's Greenhill Nursery, 2131 Vallejo Street, St. Helena, Calif. 94574. Exotic ferns.

Mrs. E. Reed Brelsford, 1816 Cherry Street, Jacksonville, Fla. 32205. Exotic ferns.

John Brudy, P.O.B. 64, Cocoa Beach, Fla. 32931. Rare shrub seeds and plants. Succulents. Seed list and plant brochure on request.

Buell's Greenhouses, Eastford, Conn. 06242. Gloxinias and other gesneriads. Catalog $1.00.

W. Atlee Burpee Co., Philadelphia, Pa. 19132. Seeds and supplies.

Milburn O. Button, Rt. 1, Box 386, Crestwood, Ky. 40014. Gesneriad seed.

Cactus by Mueller, 10411 Rosedale Highway, Bakersfield, Calif. 93307. List 10¢.

California Jungle Gardens, 11977 San Vicente Boulevard, West Los Angeles, Calif. 90049. Bromeliads and other tropicals.

Caprilands Herb Farm, Coventry, Conn. 06238. Herb seeds and plants. Lists.

Charbet Nursery, 7 Toucan Court, Wayne, N.J. 07470. Houseplants. Gesneriads. Mostly wholesale.

Chester Hills Orchids, R.R. 2, Catfish Lane, Pottstown, Pa. 19464. Orchids.

Cornelison Bromeliad Nursery, 225 San Bernardino Street, N. Fort Meyers, Fla. 33903.

Craven's Greenhouse, 4732 West Tennessee, Denver, Colo. 80219. African Violets and other gesneriads.

Dee's Garden, E-3803 19th Avenue, Spokane, Wash. 99203. Gesneriads, etc.

Desert Plant Co., Box 880, Marfa, Tex. 79843. Cactus list on request.

Dos Pueblos Orchid Company, P.O.B. 158, Goleta, Calif. 93017. Orchids—Phalaenopsis and Paphiopedilums. Catalog.

L. Easterbrook Greenhouses, Butler, Ohio 44822. African Violets and other gesneriads. Large list 50¢.

Engert's Violet House, 7457 Schuyler Drive, Omaha, Nebr. 68114. African Violets and other gesneriads.

Fantastic Gardens, 9550 S.W. 67th Avenue, South Miami, Fla. 33156. Bromeliads, ferns, exotic foliage. No shipping.

Farm & Garden Nursery, 116 Reade Street, N.Y., N.Y. 10013. Foliage plants, blooming houseplants, fixtures, supplies.

Fennell Orchid Co., Inc., 26715 S.W. 157 Avenue, Homestead, Fla. 33030. Orchids.

Susan Feece, Box 9479, Walkerton, Ind. 46574. African Violets and gesneriads.

Fischer Greenhouses, Linwood, N.J., 08221. African Violets and other gesneriads and foliage houseplants. Catalog 20¢. Also houseplant supplies catalog 50¢.

The Garden Nook, Highway No. 1, Raleigh, N.C. Exotic plants.

Gesneriad Jungle, 2507 Washington Pike, Knoxville, Tenn. 37917. Stamp for list.

Goochland Nurseries, Inc., Pembroke, Fla. 33866. Indoor plant list.

Granger Gardens, Route 2, Wilbur Road, Medina, Ohio 44256. Gesneriads. List 10¢.

Grass Roots Ltd. 8 Crestview, Bloomfield, Conn. 06002. Plants, supplies.

The Green House, 9515 Flower Street, Bellflower, Calif. 90706. African Violets, gesneriads, supplies. Fluorescent light units.

Greene Herb Gardens, Greene, R.I. 02827. List.

Greenland Flower Shop, Port Matilda, Pa. 16870. Houseplants. Catalog 25¢.

Harborcrest Nurseries, 1425 Benvenuto Avenue, Victoria, B.C., Canada. Gesneriads.

Hausermann's Orchids, Inc., Addison Road and Ninth Avenue, Elmhurst, Ill. 60126.

Henrietta's Nursery, 1345 North Brawley Avenue, Fresno, Calif. 93705. Cacti and succulents. Catalog 50¢.

Margaret Ilgenfritz, P.O.B. 665, Monroe, Mich. 48161. Orchids.

J's African Violets, 6932 Wise Avenue, St. Louis, Mo. 63139. Also supplies.

J & L Orchids, 20 Sherwood Road, Easton, Conn. 06812. Botanical orchids. Fine source.

Jones Nursery, Hazlet, N.J. 07730. Gesneriads.

Jones & Scully, 2200 N.W. 33rd Avenue, Miami, Fla. 33142. Orchids. Catalog. $1.00.

Jungle Plants & Flowers, P.O.B. 389, Culver City, Calif. 90230. Bromeliads.

Kartuz Greenhouses, 92 Chestnut Street, Wilmington, Mass. 01887. Gesneriads and begonias. Outstanding. Catalog 25¢.

Kensington Orchids Inc., 33101 Plyers Mill Road, Kensington, Md. 20795. Orchids.

Kent's Bromeliads, 6518 Bedford Avenue, Los Angeles, Calif. 90056. List 35¢.

Lager & Hurrell, 426 Morris Avenue, Summit, N.J. 07901. Orchids. Catalog (listing and cultural) $2.00.

Lauray of Salisbury, Under Mountain Road, Salisbury, Conn. 06068. Gesneriads, begonias, succulents, and other houseplants. List.

Leatherman's Gardens, 2637 N. Lee Avenue, South El Monte, Calif. 91733. Ferns.

Logee's Greenhouses, Danielson, Conn. 06239. Begonias, gesneriads, varied foliage and blooming houseplants. Catalog 50¢.

Lyndon Lyon, 14 Mutchler Street, Dolgeville, N.Y. 13329. African Violets and gesneriads. Also other houseplants. List.

Rod McLellan Co., 1450 El Camino Real, South San Francisco, Calif. 94080. Orchids. Catalog.

McComb's Greenhouses, New Straitsville, Ohio 43766. Varied houseplants.

Mary's African Violets, 19788 San Juan, Detroit, Mich. 48221. Supplies. Fluorescent fixtures.

Marz Bromeliads, 10782 Citrus Drive, Moorpark, Calif. 93021. List 20¢.

Merry Gardens, Camden, Maine 04843. Outstanding houseplants. Catalog $1.00.

New Mexico Cactus Research, P.O.B. 787, Belen, N.Mex. 87002. Cactus seed.

Novel Plants, Bridgeton, Ind. 47836. Houseplants. Catalog 10¢.

Norvell Greenhouses, 318 S. Greenacres Road, Greenacres, Wash. 99016. Varied list of foliage and blooming houseplants. Catalog 25¢.

Oakhurst Gardens, 345 Colorado Blvd., Arcadia, Calif. Carnivorous plants and exotic bulbs.

Geo. W. Park Seed Co., 64 Cokesbury Road, Greenwood, S.C. 29646. Outstanding seed catalog including many houseplants. Also plants. Catalog on request.

Payne's Violets & Gesneriads, 6612 Leavenworth Road, Kansas City, Kans. 66104.

Peter Paul's Nursery, Macedon Road, Canandaigua, N.Y. 14424. Catalog 25¢.

Plant Oddities, Box 127, Basking Ridge, N.J. 07920. Carnivorous plants. Catalog 25¢.

Quality Violet House, Box 947, Walkerton, Ind. 46574. Gesneriads.

Roehrs Exotic Nurseries, R.D. 2, Box 144, Farmingdale, N.J. 07727. Houseplants. No shipping. Roehrs's Mr. Graf is author of *Exotica*.

Mrs. Bert Routh, Lewisburg, Mo. 65685. Gesneriads.

Savage Gardens, P.O.B. 163, McMinnville, Tenn. 37110. Woodland terrarium plants. List for stamped addressed envelope.

Scotsward Violet Farm, 71 Hanover Road, Florham Park, N.J. 07932. African Violets, species.

Seaborn Del Dios Nursery, Route 3, Box 455, Escondido, Calif. 92025. Bromeliads. Catalog $1.00.

Spidell's Fine Plants, P.O.B. 93D, Junction City, Oreg. 97448. African Violets and gesneriads. List.

Taylor's Herb Garden, Rosemead, Calif. 91770.

Tinari Greenhouses, 2325 Valley Road, Huntingdon Valley, Pa. 19006. African Violets, other gesneriads, fluorescent light units. List.

Tropical Gardens, R.R. 1, Box 143, Greenwood, Ind. 46142. Houseplants.

Tropical Paradise Greenhouse, 8825 W. 79th Street, Overland Park, Kans. 66104.

Mrs. Leonard Volkart, Russelville, Mo. 65074. African Violets and Episcias.

Volkmann Bros. Greenhouses, 2714 Minert Street, Dallas, Tex. 75219. African Violets. Houseplants. Supplies.

West Coast Gesneriads, 2179 44th Avenue, San Francisco, Calif. 94116. Gesneriads. Does not ship. Fine grower.

Whistling Hill Greenhouses, Box 27, Hamburg, N.Y. 16075. Gesneriads. List.

Williford's Nursery, Rte. 3, Smithfield, N.C. 27577. Houseplants. Catalog 20¢.

Wyrtzen Exotic Plants, 165 Bryant Avenue, Floral Park, N.Y. 11001. Begonias and gesneriads. List.

Sources of Glass and Plastic Terrariums

You will find glass or plastic containers, useful for terrariums, in variety, department, and housewares stores all over the country. Because of the fad for terrariums, many glass or plastic shapes, which formerly had specialized applications, are now being displayed and sold in these places—vases, bottles, laboratory glass, and so on. In addition there are tropical fish tanks which every aquarium store sells. And now there is a flood of plastic and glass products labeled terrariums or indoor greenhouses. Usually the terrariums are in decorative shapes and the greenhouses look like small greenhouses.

Since it is no longer necessary to go to specialty stores, a list of sources is to a large extent superfluous . . . for we cannot list all the stores in the country which handle these products. The list we do give below is partly made up of large firms which sell only wholesale and whose products are available everywhere. Other firms will deal with you directly. In most large cities there are numerous manufacturers, of whom we know nothing, that make suitable plastic or glass containers. Almost any plastic molder is likely to be turning out terrarium forms for retail distribution. In other words the demand for terrariums is already engaging the activities of a great number of firms using both raw materials.

Aldermaston Sales, 25 Brookdale Road, Glen Cove, N.Y. 11542. Attractive plastic terrariums and terrarium kits. The terrariums have colored bases and clear covers. Kits contain seed of easy foliage and succulent plants.

Allgrove, Arthur Eames, North Wilmington, Mass. 01887. Plastic domes and bubbles. Bottles.

Ambassador All Glass Aquariums, Inc., 7 Dixon Avenue, Amityville,

Long Island, N.Y. 11701. Fish tanks in many sizes, with a wooden rim at the base.

Anchor Hocking Corp., 199 N. Broad Street, Lancaster, Ohio 43130. Large candy jars and other containers. Glass.

Aquarium Stock Co., Inc., 31 Warren Street, N.Y., N.Y. 10007. Tropical fish tanks. Catalog.

B. L. Designs, Inc., 354 Manhattan Avenue, Brooklyn, N.Y. 11211. Many dome, egg-shaped and bottle terrariums. Also the Mini-Terrarium. No retail.

Basic Electronics, Inc., Box 551, Danielson, Conn. 06239. Glass Coffee Table Terrarium. A deluxe terrarium with plants and running water built under a glass coffee table. Individual orders.

Blenko Glass Co., Milton, W.Va. 25541. Beautiful hand-blown vases and other containers. Wholesale representative in N.Y., Rubel & Co., 225 Fifth Avenue, N.Y., N.Y. 10012.

Bonniers, 605 Madison Avenue, N.Y. 10022. This fine store carries the Aquadome and the Stolzle Vases. Retail.

Carnival, Inc., 225 Greenwich Avenue, Greenwich, Conn. 06830. Plastic greenhouse kits.

J. C. Chester Mfg. Co., 59 Branch St., St. Louis, Mo. 63147. Plastic terrariums.

Christen Incorporated, 59 Branch St., St. Louis, Mo. 63147. Produces the Terrasphere—10- and 12-inch bubbles in two parts —and kits. Also a more expensive line of metal bases with differently shaped domes.

Corning Glass Works. Consumer Products Div., 717 Fifth Avenue, N.Y., N.Y. 10022, handles Creative Glass, a collection of modern containers for kitchen and decoration. The industrial division sells laboratory glass containers, flasks, etc.

Crystal Glass Tube & Cylinder Co., 7310 S. Chicago Avenue, Chicago, Ill. 60619. Domes and cylinders.

Dome Enterprises, 2109 Skylark, Arlington, Tex. 76010. You can buy their designs from them as Hemispheres I–III. I is the same as the Aquadome. Big, expensive, and beautiful.

Ecolibrium Industries, 61 Balsam Road, Wayne, N.J. 07470. Automated terrariums, etc.

Edelstein & Goldstein Designs, Ltd., 272 West 86th Street, N.Y., N.Y. 10024. Plastic hanging and table planters. Cubes.

Environmental Arts, 3190 Matilda Street, Coconut Grove, Fla. 33133. Terrariums. Retail.

Environmental Ceramics, 651 Howard Street, San Francisco, Calif. 95105. Terrariums.

Gould Products Inc., 791 Meacham Avenue, Elmont, N.Y. 11003. An extensive line of plastic terrariums, some sold by variety stores.

Growers Supply Co., Ann Arbor, Mich. 48103. Large plastic indoor greenhouse.

H. P. Supplies, Box 18101, Cleveland, Ohio 44118. They make a plastic cover for their light unit and kit, which turns it into a terrarium environment.

The House Plant Corner, Box 165S, Oxford, Md. 21654. Plastic terrariums and indoor greenhouses. Catalog 20¢.

John's Inc., Apopka, Fla. 32703. Plastic two-part bubble terrariums and kits with plants and soil.

Kenbury Glass Works, 154 W. 14th Street, N.Y., N.Y. 10011. Glass domes, cylinders, etc.

Libby-Owens-Ford Glass Co., 99 Park Avenue, N.Y., N.Y. 10017. Container glass.

Lucidity, Inc., 959 Second Avenue and 775 Madison Avenue, N.Y., N.Y. Plastic bubbles, domes, and cubes. Retail.

Markatos-Dimitri, 1240 Madison Avenue, at 89th Street, N.Y., N.Y. 10028. Planted terrariums of quality. Retail.

Mastercraft Medical and Industrial Corp., 15–25 126th Street, College Point, N.Y. 11356. Plastic domes.

Metaframe Corporation, Slater Drive, East Paterson, New Jersey 07407. Tropical fish tanks.

Owens-Illinois Glass Co., Toledo, Ohio 43601. Glass containers.

Geo. W. Park Seed Co., Greenwood, S.C. 29467. Domes, bubbles, indoor greenhouses. Catalog.

Plexi-Craft, 195 Chrystie Street, N.Y., N.Y. 10002. Plastic cubes and cylinders.

Raja Toy Company, 1206 South La Jolla Avenue, Los Angeles, Calif. 90035. Most complete line of plastic domes and indoor greenhouses with kits. Catalog and cultural handbook available.

Riekes-Crisa, Omaha, Nebr. 68102. N.Y.C. representative 225 Fifth Avenue, N.Y., N.Y. 10010. Outstanding hand-blown glass terrariums, snifters, bubbles, globes, bottles, etc. Handsome and not expensive.

West Virginia Glass Co., Weston, West Virginia 26452. Glass bubbles in all sizes.

Where to Purchase Equipment and Supplies

American Plant Food Co., Inc., 5258 River Road, Bethesda, Md. Fluorescent tubes, plant supplies, fertilizers.

Aquarium Stock Co. Inc., 31 Warren Street, N.Y., N.Y. 10007. Glass tanks, algicides, water purifiers, pumps, etc.

Atlas Fish Emulsion Fertilizer, Menlo Park, Calif. 94025.

Baccto Organic Peat, One Decker Square, Suite 325, Bala-Cynwyd, Pa. 19004. Peat moss and peat mixes.

Black Magic Inc., 530 Sixth Street, Hermosa Beach, Calif. 90254. Houseplant soils.

Commercial Plastics & Supply Corp., 630 Broadway, N.Y., N.Y.
    10012. Plastic domes, cubes, etc.
Frank Crea, 1274 Adee Avenue, Bronx, N.Y. 10469. Tabletop fix-
    tures, fluorescent lights.
Do-Ja-Ma Flower & Specialty Shop, P.O. Box 297, Middletown,
    N.Y. 10940. Terrariums and planters.
Emerson Industries, Inc., Hempstead, Long Island, N.Y. Glass
    Wardian Cases with fluorescent lights. Window greenhouses.
Flora Greenhouses, Box 1191, Burlingame, Calif. 94010. Fluo-
    rescent fixtures.
Floralite Co., 4124 E. Oakwood Rd., Oak Creek, Wis. 53154. Fluo-
    rescent plant stands of several types.
Friendly Gardeners Inc., Box One, Lake Oswego, Oreg. 97034.
    High phosphate and potash fertilizer "Sturdy."
The Green House, 9515 Flower Street, Bellflower, Calif. 90706.
    Tiered fluorescent units.
Bernard J. Greeson, 3548 N. Cramer St., Milwaukee, Wis. 53211.
    Equipment and supplies. List 10¢.
A. H. Hoffman, Inc., Landisville, Pa. 17538. Fertilizers and prepared
    mixes.
The House Plant Corner, Box 165, Oxford, Md. 21654. All kinds
    of supplies and equipment.
Hydroponic Chemical Company, Copley, Ohio 44321. Fertilizers.
Industrial Plastic Supply Co., 324 Canal Street, N.Y., N.Y. 10013.
    Plastic domes, cubes, etc.
International Register Co., 2624 W. Washington Boulevard, Chicago,
    Ill. 60612. Intermatic brand time controls.
Lifelite Incorporated, 1025 Shary Circle, Concord, Calif. 94520.
    Fluorescent lighting equipment.
Lighting Inc., P.O.B. 2228, Raleigh, N.C. 27602. Lighting equip-
    ment.
Mosser Lee, Millston, Wis. 54643. Sphagnum moss.
The Natural Development Co., Box 215, Bainbridge, Pa. 17502.
    Fish fertilizer, organic insecticides.
Neas Growers Supply Co., P.O.B. 8773, Greenville, S.C. 29604.
    Fluorescent equipment, supplies.
Norran Inc., 14957 Lakewood Heights Boulevard, Cleveland, Ohio
    44107. Tiered fluorescent light unit.
Paragon Time Control, Inc., Three Rivers, Wisc. Timers. Astro-
    nomic timers.
Geo W., Park Seed Co., Inc., Greenwood, S.C. 29646. Fluorescent
    equipment, supplies, seeds. Catalog.
Robt. W. Peters Co., Inc., 2833 Pennsylvania St., Allentown, Pa.
    18104. Fertilizers.
Plant Marvel Laboratories, W. 119 Street, Chicago, Ill. 60628.
    Fertilizers.
Rolling Stones, Inc., Franklin, Mich. 48025. Sisal pot holders.

Al Saffer & Co., Inc., 130 West 28th Street, N.Y., N.Y. 10001. Extensive catalog of equipment and supplies for nurseries and houseplant growers.

Shoplite Co., 566 J. Franklin, Nutley, N.J. 07110. Fluorescent equipment of all kinds. Catalog 25¢.

South Shore Floral Co., 1050 Quentin Place, Woodmere, N.Y. 11598. Indoor gardening supplies. List.

Tropical Plant Products, Inc. P.O.B. 7754, Orlando, Fla. 32804. Orchid media, fertilizers, indoor gardening supplies.

Fred A. Veith, 3505 Mozart Avenue, Cincinnati, Ohio 45211. German peat moss, fertilizers, potting soils, etc.

Index